PRAISE FOR *COLLABORATE*

"There's a secret, sometimes silent struggle that creeps into all the work we do as entrepreneurs and creators...this struggle can be lethal to your business if you don't find a solution. The struggle? Trying to do everything by yourself. The solution? Collaboration.

It's easy as a business owner to slip into isolation; disconnected from others, struggling to solve a problem from personal experience alone, and, ultimately adrift in a sea of too many possibilities. Yet, when we choose to collaborate, when we connect and work with other experts to turn our idea into reality, what follows is a better product, more revenue, more fulfillment and, most importantly, more positive impact on those we choose to serve.

Tom Morkes' Collaborate provides a powerful framework for making collaboration work in your business. Collaborate is a thoroughly empowering, helpful, and practical deep-dive into a topic that answers the plight of the struggling solopreneur, and shows that there is a better, faster, more enjoyable way to create."

- **Bruce Brodeen**, founder and President of Kick Ass Publishing

"Collaboration has been the cornerstone to my professional success, and now, with Collaborate, anyone can take advantage. Tom's thoughtful and deliberate approach shines through in this step-by-step guide to collaboration, clearly written by a true subject matter expert. It's a must read (and MUST DO) for anyone looking to make a bigger impact through their work."

- **Kevin Kermes**, author, entrepreneur, speaker

"Tom Morkes reveals the secrets to succeeding in a market where collaboration is key. His case studies and testimonials are changing the way I operate. After reading Collaborate, you'll never try to go it alone again."

- **Jason B. Ladd**, author of *One of the Few*

"Tom Morkes' Collaborate offers a stark reminder that to achieve success, we do not need to go it alone. In fact, from combat missions over Afghanistan to the formation of a business - when lives, careers, and dreams are on the line - we must not go it alone!"

- **Capt Marc Aalderink**, USAF

"Collaborate is the book I have been waiting for; the wealth of its detailed, practical content; personal examples and those of proven experts; step-by-step directions and guidance; practical exercises with periodic azimuth checks; and not to mention the bonus resources... all are valuable to me both for my digital, online products, as well as my offline collaboration. As he always does, Tom Morkes has over-delivered."

- **Bob McCall**, publishing consultant

"If you are starting a collaborative project, this book should be on your bookshelf."

- **Jane Manthorpe**, author

"Collaborate is a brilliant guide for anyone approaching a collaborative venture. I recommend this especially for solopreneurs who are struggling to get traction."

- **Tathra Street**, leadership and team consultant

COLLABORATE

ALSO BY TOM MORKES

The Art of Instigating

The Complete Guide to Pay What You Want Pricing

Notes From Seth Godin's Revolution Conference

COLLABORATE

The Modern Playbook for
Leading a Small Team to Create,
Market, and Sell Digital Products Online

TOM MORKES

Published in the United States by Insurgent Publishing, LLC.
PO Box 8043, Aspen, CO 81612
www.insurgentpublishing.com

Ordering Information:

Insurgent Publishing books are available at special discounts for bulk purchases for sales promotions or corporate use. Special editions, including personalized covers, excerpts of existing books, or books with corporate logos, can be created in large quantities upon request. For more information, please contact the publisher by email at admin@insurgentpublishing.com.

Publisher's Cataloging-in-Publication Data

Names: Morkes, Tom.
Title: Collaborate : the modern playbook for leading a small team to create, market, and sell digital
products online / Tom Morkes.
Description: Aspen, CO : Insurgent Publishing, 2016. | Includes bibliographical references.
Identifiers: LCCN 2015919698 | ISBN 978-1-940715-02-5 (pbk.) | ISBN 978-1-940715-04-9 (hardcover)
Subjects: LCSH: New products--Marketing. | Electronic commerce. | Teams in the workplace. |
Entrepreneurship.| Selling.
Classification: LCC HF5415.153 .M675 2016 (print) DDC: 658.8--dc23.

Printed in the United States of America
10 9 8 7 6 5 4 3 2 1

DEDICATION

For Courtney, because I couldn't have asked for a better collaborator, in business or life.

CONTENTS

SPECIAL THANKS

I can't think of a more appropriate way to start this book than by thanking the people who made it possible: my early adopters. You took a chance on an idea and pre-ordered *Collaborate* when it was nothing more than a few words on a sales page. *Collaborate* literally wouldn't exist without you. Thank you from the bottom of my heart for your support and your patience:

Marc Aalderink
Anne Jenett
Alexandre Marcondes
Alexis Grant
Alison Crosthwait
Anne Waldon
Anthony Vennare
Adrian Hoppel
Damian Taafe-McMenamy
Benjamin Loh
Beth O'Donnell
Barbara Mistic
Bjork Ostrom
Steve Blight
Robert McCall
Brian Baulch
Bruce Brodeen
Chad Grills
C J Westwood
Larry Taylor
Matthew Miller
David Papa
Deacon Bradley
Doug Hibbard
Denise Wakeman
Don Alexander
Doug Geiger
Dan Morkes
Elisa Doucette
Eugene Adams
Fabian Schmidt
Fadhilah Wahid
Frank Gustafson
Gary Auerbach
Grace Conyers
Gia Combs-ramirez
Giovanna Beltrão
Giuseppe Fratoni
Greg Spiro
Guy Vincent

Hilary Barrett
Hari Simaguen
Andrew Nixon
Anfernee Chansamooth
Zaid Ansari
Tai Whyte
Jason B. Ladd
Jesica Carlo
Juan Barrios
Jane Manthorpe
Jeff Rose
John Blodgett
Joey Morkes
Jon Nastor
John Heaton
John Corcoran
Joshua Arcurio
Jenny Clark
Kathleen Hartmann
Katrina Tan
Kevin Kermes
Kevin Wood
Ken Chiavone
Lawrence Green
Lily Sahiful Bahari
Linda Warner
Lisa Landtroop
Laurie McCarriar
Martin Weiss
Mary Bradley
Matthew Turner
David Gran
Michael Hellerslien
Mick Hall
Martyn Bromley
Mike Needham
Niel Malhotra
Bob Newberry
Patricia BT
Peter Hellerfelt
Daniel Puglisi
Carol Gunby
Dave Chesson
Rick Roesler
Rob Williger
Ryan Guina
Ryan Hanley
Steve Clancy
Sergio Sala
Skywalker Payne
Sam M
Stacy Burrell
Stefan Vogel
Brian White
Tasha Moody-Love
Tathra Street
Tom Doughty
Noah Gibbs
Jacqui Treagus
Tyson Adams
Vanessa Sancho Morales
Wendy Poling
Wang Yip

FOREWORD

In 2013, my friend Antonio Centeno and I began brainstorming the development of a new platform that would help veterans become entrepreneurs. As veterans and established business owners ourselves, we wanted to find a way to help veterans build successful, meaningful businesses without experiencing the same pitfalls we had experienced trying to figure it out on our own.

However, while we were confident in the value proposition of our platform, we knew that neither of us had the bandwidth to make this thing a reality. EOFire.com had just hit its first million listeners and my team was at full capacity, and Antonio's business was also hitting new growth records; neither of us could take lead on this project. If we wanted to bring this idea to life, we needed someone to take the reigns.

That's when we found Tom Morkes.

Tom is a prior West Point grad, Iraq War veteran, and, when I first met him, not only was he an active duty officer getting ready to transition into the civilian world (the "target audience" for our platform), but he was already operating a blog and bootstrapping a publishing company. Clearly, he was capable of starting something from scratch, understood the online business world, and had the hustle to manage and lead multiple projects at once. After an intro call, it became clear to Antonio and I that we needed Tom on our team to make this idea a reality.

Flash forward to today and what started as a far-flung idea has turned into a leading resource for veterans looking to start or grow a business, and our premium business coaching program, High Speed Elite, has graduated three classes and is still going strong.

I've since collaborated with Tom on other projects, including the launch of TheFreedomJournal.com, a hardcover Journal that will guide you in setting and accomplishing your #1 goal in 100-days. Tom's ability to organize and lead small, collaborative teams to launch products online is the single element I was looking for when I undertook this project. Collaborating with Tom has been a no-brainer because of this.

That's why I'm so excited about *Collaborate*. When I heard Tom had taken his experience leading the creation and launch of High Speed Elite (and a number of other collaborative projects) and synthesized his learning into a framework anyone could use, I knew it would be a must read for anyone looking to build and launch an online business.

In *Collaborate*, Tom will show you the exact step-by-step process to assemble, organize, and lead a team to create, market, and sell a digital product online.

Collaborate starts, as it should, with mindset. In Phase 1, you will come to understand collaboration in a new way, define your superpower, and, most importantly, recognize where you can add value to any project regardless of your current experience level. If you've ever questioned your talents or doubted your abilities, this section will help you break through the barriers that have been holding you back.

In Phase 2, you will learn how to create a profitable idea from scratch (or test your original idea to make sure it is profitable), define and understand your ideal collaborator, and step-by-step instructions on how to get them to join your team. For anyone who has avoided collaboration because the idea of finding and connecting with the right teammates seems intimidating, this section is for you.

In Phase 3, you will learn how to collaboratively create your product, from establishing Standard Operating Procedures your entire team can embrace, to properly planning your project and timeline, to building your Minimal Viable Product. Whether you're part of a large or small team, this section is required reading for anyone looking to creating and launch a digital product.

In Phase 4, you will learn how to build a simple, yet effective sales funnel from scratch, use it to build an audience, and, most importantly, pre-sell your product before you ever create it. This is lean business at its core and something I personally embrace: I never start a new project without a massive pre-sale campaign. Warning: this Phase may change the way you do business forever.

In Phase 5, you'll learn how to take your new audience, new pre-orders, and new platform and begin to build your product or service through collaborative crowdsourcing. You'll also learn how to effectively onboard new customers so they become your biggest fans (and best word-of-mouth referral engine on the planet). Finally, you'll learn how to conduct a proper After Action Review, something I used in my time in the U.S. Army to properly analyze, review, and learn from all of our missions and training exercises.

Like a good General, Tom has developed a simple, yet powerful strategy that anyone can follow to create a better product or service, and get it to market faster, while prioritizing your goals and the lifestyle you want to live.

My advice: get *Collaborate* (a few copies: for yourself and for the people you intend to work with), read it, do the exercises together, take and compare notes, put your learning into action, and prepare to IGNITE your business and life.

—John Lee Dumas, CEO of EOFire.com LLC

John Lee Dumas is the founder and host of EOFire, an award winning Podcast where he interviews today's most inspiring Entrepreneurs 7-days a week. JLD has produced over 1000 episodes and EOFire generates $300,000 a month in revenue. With over 1 million unique monthly listens, EOFire has inspired Fire Nation to face their fears and take the Entrepreneurial leap!

INTRODUCTION

Steve is an electrical engineer with a decent salary and a loving family. He's not unhappy with his work, but he's overheard rumors of a new wave of company-wide layoffs. Naturally, he's nervous. Steve doesn't want to quit his job or uproot his family by taking a new position somewhere else, so he's looking to make money on the side. He's heard the internet is an easy place to make money (or so they say), and he gets started.

Steve spends the first few weeks of his foray into online business purchasing training programs and learning everything there is to know about blogging, social media, email marketing, WordPress, widgets, and more. Because Steve is doing this on the side, a few weeks of study turns into a few months (Steve is a very analytical person and likes to know everything before beginning work). Finally, Steve is ready to put his knowledge into action. The problem is that Steve isn't exactly sure what he wants to build. So he spends another three months tweaking his website until he has something he likes.

Once Steve has his website up and running, he reads about content marketing, and is told that to build a business online, you need to create content. So Steve starts a blog and begins writing about electrical engineering (he's told to teach what he knows and he starts there). He also reads that you're supposed to share your work through social media, so he creates a Twitter account, G+ account, Instagram account, and Facebook Page. After a month of writing and promoting his work on social media (which takes much more time than Steve expected), Steve is disappointed to learn his blog is only getting about 10 viewers a day. Undeterred, Steve keeps writing because several people he knows working online have said that's just how it is in the beginning and the best thing to do is stick it out.

After a few months of writing, Steve is now comfortable publishing on his blog, but he has yet to make a single dollar from his work. In fact, he's a few thousand in the hole because of the initial investment into tools, training, and software to get this far. While Steve's "list building" efforts are slow, he keeps the faith. He reads a popular, new article online that tells him his biggest problem is not having a product to sell, so Steve buys the corresponding course that will teach him to build a product, and gets to work.

The course is useful, but it's slow moving for Steve. Pressure is building at work because of the layoffs and he has less time to devote to his project. His wife is upset he's spent so many hours (and so much money) on this hobby and it's not showing any returns. Steve is annoyed at himself for not working faster, and decides it's because his process isn't efficient enough. So Steve picks up a new training program on how to set up systems and processes that will help him "scale" his business.

Steve quickly realizes that in order to scale systems, he needs people to help him. Steve decides to pick up a new book about outsourcing, which excites him. While Steve hasn't made any money from his side project just yet, he loves the idea that he can get a part-time employee for only a few hundred dollars a month. So Steve doubles down on his effort and hires a full-time Virtual Assistant that can help him scale his business.

After two months of teaching his Virtual Assistant everything about his current business, Steve gets back to work on building a new product. He starts by outlining his product, which teaches people how to become electrical engineers in their spare time. Building the product takes longer than expected because Steve's Virtual Assistant follows instructions word-for-word, so he needs to spend extra time creating simple instructions for his VA to execute—and that doesn't help him with the creative aspect of the product, including content development, marketing material development, etc. Steve realizes a VA is nice for small, simple, repetitive tasks, but won't help him actually build his product. He's on his own.

Finally, after hundreds of hours of effort, Steve finishes his new product—a training course for aspiring electrical engineers. The course took even longer than expected because he had to set up a new membership system, integrate payment gateways, and incorporate his business into an LLC. But now, Steve is ready to share his product with the world.

Steve creates a blog post about his new course. *Nothing happens.*

He then shares it on social media. *Crickets.*

Finally, he emails his list of 200 newsletter subscribers. *Two sales.*

Steve hopes it's just a side-effect of sharing on a Monday, so he tries again later in the week. One or two more sales trickle in. After a couple weeks of "launching" his product, it occurs to Steve that he has now spent over a year building something that has resulted in only a few hundred dollars in revenue—not nearly enough to pay for his current expenses, let alone compensate him for the time he spent building.

There has to be a better way....

A better way to start, finish, and ship your project

This book is designed as an actionable playbook for struggling solopreneurs to show them a better, faster, more rewarding way to create, market, and sell digital products online. In *Collaborate*, I'll show you how to lead a small team of experts by leveraging cheap technology, remote work systems and processes, and cutting-edge online marketing strategies.

In other words, I'm going to teach you how to *collaborate.*

My goal with this book is to help you avoid the trap that Steve in our story fell into (and that so many people I've known have fallen into without even realizing it). You see, Steve didn't do everything wrong. In fact, he did a lot of stuff right, which we will cover in this book. But he ultimately failed because he ignored a few critical principles of life and business.

First, everything suffers from time decay. Time decay is a term commonly used in options trading. It refers to the value that is lost as an options contract gets closer to expiration. In other words, the longer it takes us to do something, the more value we lose in the process. Put another way—speed is critical for your success. If you want to succeed at starting a business online, you can't afford to spend two years building. That's why this book will help you create, market, and sell your first digital product in 30 days.

Second, the 80/20 principle is ever present in everything we do, both in business and life. The 80/20 principle, or the Pareto Principle, states that essentially everything in life is not equally distributed, but rather 80% of results stem from just 20% of our efforts. Put another way, there are certain activities that create very little value (about 80% of what we do is low value). Conversely, there are a few, select activities that produce the majority of our results. This is true in any area, whether in product development, marketing, sales, etc. In this book, I want to show you the 20% of activities that will produce 80% of the results (and revenue), even if this means doing things that seem unconventional, contrarian, or uncomfortable—because by their nature, they will be.

Lastly, human beings were not built to live, work, and play alone. No great work was ever created in a vacuum. Humans are social creatures by nature, and when you try to do everything by yourself, you cut off a certain power only accessible to those in tight-knit, small groups working toward a collective goal. If you've ever been a part of a club, sports team, or had a few best friends growing up, then you probably know what I mean; there's nothing that beats having a brother-in-arms to share your victories, or comfort you in times of loss. This is as true in the military as it is in business. In this book, I'll show you how to let go of being a loner and how to become a teammate, a leader, and a collaborator.

What this book is not...

There have been many books written on the topic of collaboration from a conceptual and creative standpoint: *Collaboration* by Morten Hansen, *The Power of Two* by Joshua Wolf, *Collaboration Economy* by John Spencer Ellis and Topher Morrison, *Reinventing Discovery* by Michael Nielsen, and *Creative Conspiracy* by Leigh Thompson, just to name a few. These books are entertaining and educational. I've drawn a lot of inspiration from these books to write the one you're currently reading, and I encourage anyone interested in the topic of collaboration to add them to your reading list. Yet, while these books answer the question "why collaborate?" they don't show us *how*—and certainly not in the context of online business.

That's why *Collaborate: The Modern Playbook for Leading a Small Team to Create, Market, and Sell Digital Products Online* takes a different approach:

#1. It is not theoretical

The frameworks, strategies, and processes covered here have been used by myself and thousands of other entrepreneurs, artists, and writers around the world to achieve incredible results in a short period of time. While there is always room for improvement, what you read and learn here does work. These skills just need to be applied in a specific way and a particular order. This book will show you how.

#2. It is not general

Collaboration itself is an extensive subject. Many of the books mentioned earlier have already explored the topic in broad brush strokes. This is why I've chosen to focus on collaborative online business development, specifically focusing on product launches.

This means I'll show you:

- ✓ How to brainstorm and develop your idea
- ✓ How to find and connect with experts online
- ✓ How to collaboratively turn your idea into a working business model,
- ✓ How to progressively build your product remotely (using cost-effective online tools and resources), and finally...
- ✓ How to launch your product to create the greatest reach, impact, and sales possible.

By its nature, the act of narrow focus means this book isn't for everybody. It's not supposed to be. The good news is I didn't write this for everybody. I wrote it for you. I hope you enjoy.

#3. It is not a panacea for a bad product or poor execution

While I'll do my best to show you the framework and process to develop, build, and launch a profitable project, there are still many opportunities to fail. If you build a product nobody wants or your execution is subpar, no amount of collaboration can save you.

Collaboration is exponential—it compounds the actions you take and the results you create. This is a double-edged sword; it means you can create better, faster results, more efficiently than by working on your own...but it also means the potential failure is bigger because more people are now involved in the project (so if your project doesn't pan out, it's not just you who will hurt, but your collaborators).

Here's the thing: creating anything worthwhile takes work. There are no shortcuts here and I don't promise any. Instead, I'm simply providing you the roadmap to build a better product, faster, more enjoyably, and with greater financial upside than going it alone. As long as you're willing to put in the work, you can reap the benefits yourself.

Six reasons to start collaborating today

While I've alluded to why collaboration is better than working as a solopreneur, it's worth our time to understand precisely why this is the case. The following are the six most important reasons you should begin collaborating today:

#1. Build a better product

If you are a writer, is your reader best served by you formatting, marketing, packaging, and distributing your own book? Or is your reader best served by having experts in those areas do those things for you, while you focus on what only you can do—writing?

If you're an entrepreneur, is your customer best served by you building each widget by hand personally, or is your customer better served by you leveraging talented people and cheap technology to engineer a better, less expensive product that can reach more people?

If you're an artist, are your biggest fans best served by you fulfilling and shipping each print order, or by you producing your best work—what only you can do—the actual act of painting?

You get the point.

Fundamentally, this is a question of talent used to best effect. When you try to do everything yourself, you must, by necessity, do things where you do not excel. This means some elements of what you produce won't be as good as they could be had you leveraged the skills of others in these areas.

By collaborating, you'll find the best people to work with—people with skills that you don't have (or who are simply better in a particular area)—so that you can focus on your core competency. The result? A better product for the customer.

How Martyn Bromley is building a better product through collaboration

According to Martyn Bromley, CEO and founder of Herosite.co, "no business is an island."

His web development company helps clients turn their skills into profitable online businesses. However, as a small, but growing company, Bromley doesn't have the resources to hire a full staff. Instead, he relies on collaboration to deliver a remarkable end product:

"In terms of collaboration, I am trying to build that deeply into the heart of Herosite.co so that I can get a group of independent experts to work together to help one another grow our businesses. For me, I have my own weaknesses; I am terrible at copywriting. When I first started developing websites for clients, I knew the copywriting wasn't good enough. Because I was on a budget, my only option was to work collaboratively with other experts. To make this happen, I have actually traded time and skills with people. Bartering has become a great way for me to deal with other businesses while still delivering for my customers. For example, at Herosite.co we develop, design, and code other people's websites, but then I'll often collaborate with a copywriter to finish off the site."

When asked about working collaboratively versus working alone, Bromley had this to say: "Working alone just grinds you down after a while. That's why I've been trying to form bands of people together to get them to work together on one another's businesses, leveraging the strengths of each individual person. I actually have the quote 'no business is an island' pinned above my laptop right now."

#2. Create faster and more efficiently

As a solopreneur, if you run into a problem with the backend technology of your website, what do you do? One option is to hire a contractor to fix it for you. The problem here is that if you have no idea what the problem is, you can't properly estimate how much it should reasonably cost, nor how long it should take. If you go this route, you may end up paying a premium, with no guarantee that the solution will work at all.

Alternatively, you could try fixing it yourself. If you go this route, you can be sure no shortcuts are made that could compromise the final product. Unfortunately, the do-it-yourself approach has a way of stealing hours of your life, often expanding into a much bigger task than you envisioned at the outset. Worse still, there's no guarantee you'll actually find the right solution. If that turns out to be the case, you're back to option one, but this time you've wasted hours (days?) of your time you could have spent doing higher-value activities.

Neither choice is ideal when you're bootstrapping a project (bootstrapping = building something on a limited budget, without outside investment).

Luckily, when you collaborate there's a third option: leverage your collaborative partner who excels in this area, who is invested in the project, and who wants the same results as you. This will allow you to create faster (no need to hire out the solution or try to figure things out yourself), more rewardingly (no more struggling with painful tasks or managing a contractor who doesn't care about your business), while reducing waste (waste of time, money, or effort).

How Guy Vincent is building a faster, more efficient startup

Guy Vincent is the CEO and founder of Publishizer.com, a book pre-order platform. The goal of Publishizer.com is to give authors a platform to launch pre-order campaigns, gain traction for their book, and ultimately to rally creators and supporters around a project in a collaborative fashion. As you can imagine, he needs to coordinate with many different people from different fields to get the job done.

In terms of organizing his startup, Guy works with several freelancers, all of whom work full time jobs outside of Publishizer.com. This requires Guy to take an autonomous approach to accomplishing his business goals:

"Basically, I tell my collaborators: here's what we want to accomplish, this is why we want to accomplish it, go ahead and do whatever you want to accomplish that, because I trust you."

Guy's reasoning is simple: "I let people thrive on the work that they're great at. So I always let them just focus purely on what they do best, which, for the people I'm coordinating with to build Publishizer.com, is back-end and front-end engineering, and I let them solve the problems in the ways that they want to solve them."

Guy has done such a remarkable job building Publishizer.com that he was invited to attend 500 Startups during the summer 2015 batch (what they call a new group of tech startup incubation students).

Getting accepted into 500 Startups is hyper competitive and a testament to Guy's ability to get the most out of people through the power of collaboration.

#3. Multiply your results

Beyond creating better products more rapidly and efficiently, collaboration will help you compound your results. Simple arithmetic tells us that 1+1=2. Therefore, you might believe that bringing on a partner would merely double your results. This is not the case. When applied to real world projects, the combination of two experts with complementary but different skillsets, is much less like addition and much more like an exponential factor—something more akin to: $(1+1)^2=4$.

For example, if you're great at writing, but not great at web design, it may take you days to develop a website that it would take a competent designer just hours to create. By removing yourself as the bottleneck and leveraging someone else with a particular skillset in web design, you can more than double the speed of production. If you're able to double your production rate, this means you can ship your product to market sooner, meaning you'll be able to realize your gains sooner, thus moving onto the next project faster than had you tried to do it all by yourself. Over time, this creates a hockey stick-style curve on a graph because you are compounding your results, one after another.

Case Study: How The Flight Formula generated over $40,000 in revenue from a part-time collaboration

One of the first collaborative projects I worked on was a business incubator program called The Flight Formula. The program itself was a one week, intensive, in-person business mastermind and incubation experience, with the goal of helping a small group of entrepreneurs get their businesses off the ground and running.

In order to get the program up and running rapidly, we coordinated specific activities each person would be in charge of; one person was in charge of creating the website, another the ecommerce backend, while I focused on marketing and sales. The end result was a 5-figure launch that we were able to coordinate remotely (I was traveling around South Africa during the launch). Because of our initial success, we were able to launch a digital program immediately afterward, resulting in several thousand more dollars in revenue just weeks later (versus months).

Two important points to take away from this story: first, I simply could not have done this without the help of others to coordinate other aspects of the program, like actually running it in person. Second, this was an important springboard to get me started working with many other people on various collaborative projects, faster and with better results than I would have been capable of producing on my own. People are drawn to success, so the earlier you can succeed, the better off you will be in the long run. Collaboration can help you get there.

#4. Grow as an individual

You may have heard the Biblical passage: "As iron sharpens iron, so one person sharpens another." —Proverbs 27:17.

This is certainly true in the context of collaboration.

Up until now, I've only talked about the importance of collaboration in terms of the people you serve (your audience), the product you create, and your team of collaborators. But collaboration has an even more compelling benefit: it helps you become better in business by improving your personal performance.

First, when you collaborate, you have the opportunity to work with great people who can push you to do your best. Working with others, especially those who are more talented in certain areas than you, has a natural spillover effect; it forces you to improve your game, to rise to meet the occasion.[1]

Second, when you collaborate you have the opportunity to learn and grow more rapidly. Stuck on a problem? A collaborator can shine a spotlight on things you might otherwise miss if you were working alone. It's important to note that this is something employees, strangers, or even friends aren't able to replicate because they don't have the same level of investment in your project that a collaborator would have. Collaborators have the unique advantage of understanding the project and problems intimately. This can only happen in small, tight-knit groups working toward a collective goal.[2]

#5. Launch from nothing

This is arguably the "killer app" feature of collaboration. When you leverage the power of collaboration, you don't need funding, or a network, or decades of experience to create and sell a product. Instead, you can work with your collaborative partners to build the simplest version of your product, pre-sell it to your biggest fans, and then build it with their input. This is the exact process used by creators when they sell on Kickstarter, Indiegogo, or other crowdfunding campaigns, and it's a strategy that every business should use to create products faster and better, while mitigating the risk of creating something nobody wants.

Starting from scratch with Publishizer.com

A few months into developing Publishizer, Guy Vincent ran into a common problem experienced by bootstrapped business owners: he ran out of money.

For most solopreneurs, this is the end of the story. For those who choose to collaborate, there are options. Here's what happened to Vincent in his own words:

"I ran out of money; I spent all that I could afford to get the minimum viable product up and ready to launch a few book pre-order campaigns. These early campaigns were successful, so I knew there was potential. I told Martin and Toby, the two engineers I had originally hired to build Publishizer.com: 'Guys, I'm out of cash. I'll do my best to make this platform work with what we've got.' And they said, 'Look, this is actually pretty fun for us, we enjoy working on it, it's a fun side project—if you give us equity, we can continue working on it with you.' To which, I was like, 'Hell yeah!' So that was when they came on board and joined the team, and yeah, we've been collaborating on the platform ever since."

Guy was able to grow Publishizer.com into a successful venture in spite of running out of funds because he was able to negotiate a collaborative working arrangement with his engineers.

#6. Avoid the loneliness and despair of solopreneurship

On the topic of loneliness and despair, I can only share my personal experience. Perhaps this isn't a bad thing, though, as according to statistician and risk analyst Nassim Taleb:"Experience is devoid of the cherry-picking that we find in studies."[3]

I've been fortunate enough to work by myself on dozens of projects, and as a collaborator on multiple projects, from books, to blogs, to businesses—the latter, only with fervor and consistency in the past three years. Up until that point, almost every project was a solo endeavor. I can say for certain: while I'm proud of what I've created, the road of solitary creation is long and lonely. Most days I felt like quitting. And because I didn't have a teammate to back me up, sometimes I did.

It begs the question:

1. What was lost because I didn't get outside my own head?
2. What could have become of those projects that failed because I was too proud to seek others who were better than me to work alongside?
3. What opportunities to positively impact the world were missed because I didn't work with others?

Humans weren't made to live, work, or play alone. We were made to connect with others and co-create. This process gives every person strength, energy, and courage. When you work alone, you cut yourself off from this power that can truly elevate your work.

No great work was ever created in a vacuum.

Get outside the house (and your head) and start collaborating.

How Corbett Barr built Fizzle.co with collaboration in mind from the start

Corbett Barr, CEO and co-founder of Fizzle.co, began as a self-proclaimed lone wolf. Like many aspiring entrepreneurs, he started building online businesses as a solopreneur. And like many solopreneurs, he found the "solo" venture simply too taxing and too slow.

"There's a lot of reasons to think that solopreneurship is really sexy and, for certain reasons, it is. But after a few years of not taking any vacations, you start to wonder how sexy is this life that I'm living, really, because I have to do everything. For example, say you go on vacation and you have all of your blog posts or whatever scheduled in advance, there could still be a crisis. Your website could go down, or some customers could have some issues and get really angry about it. There's all kinds of things that can happen. So, you just don't necessarily feel comfortable enough to step away entirely. Another thing you start to realize as a solopreneur is that you don't have all the skills to make everything happen that you want to happen. You can't necessarily build your whole vision based on just the skills that you have. And finally, solopreneurship starts to get a little lonely and a little boring after awhile."

While Barr started out as a solopreneur, he eventually connected with other solopreneurs online, including Chase Reeves and Caleb Wojcik, who eventually teamed up with him to co-found their premium business training platform, Fizzle.co.

How to use this book

Phases

This book is broken down into the five phases. Each phase represents a particular aspect of collaboration, specifically in the context of creating, marketing, and selling a digital product online. These five phases are:

PHASE 1: FUEL—personally prepare for the collaborative process

PHASE 2: ASSEMBLE—develop your profitable idea, and then identify, locate, and assemble your team of experts

PHASE 3: CREATE—turn your idea into a working business model, develop your plan, and begin collaboratively building

PHASE 4: LAUNCH—leverage the 80/20 principle, lean business methodology, and advanced internet marketing strategies to launch your product with a bang

PHASE 5: ACCELERATE—turn early success into sustainable revenue

Milestones

Within each Phase are a series of Milestones, organized chronologically, from start to finish. These Milestones represent the achievement of a collection of important tasks or objectives. The purpose of these Milestones is to keep you on track and on target, starting from scratch and moving along the path to shipping your product to market. Within each Milestone, you'll find a checklist of key tasks, a framework or blueprint to follow to achieve the Phase objective, step-by-step directions for executing certain tasks, and exercises to help you put your knowledge to work.

Azimuth Checks

At the end of each Milestone is an Azimuth Check. An azimuth check is a term used in the U.S. Army when a soldier is conducting land navigation. Specifically, it refers to finding where you are in respect to where you want to be, and answers the important question "are you headed in the right direction?" The Azimuth Checks in this book serve the same purpose.

While it might be tempting to gloss over the exercises or Azimuth Check within each lesson, I encourage you to complete each task, item, or exercise immediately upon reading them. The simple reason is that we all learn faster and more effectively, not from reading, but from application—these exercises will help you apply the lessons in each Milestone so you can learn and master the material.

Bonus resources

Nothing would make me happier than seeing the next book in this space inspired by your innovative application of the framework, tools, and processes found in this book. If you put this book into practice and experience great results, please share your story with me. I love seeing people succeed and would love to include your story in future editions of *Collaborate* (with your permission, of course).

That said, collaboration is not easy, and this book can't hope to cover every potential obstacle you could run into on your journey. That's why I've put together a collection of resources, tools, and bonus materials to help you better implement what you learn in this book.

You can get free access to all the bonus material at:

www.tommorkes.com/collaborate.

Finally, if after reading the book and using the bonus materials above, you still struggle with understanding or implementing these concepts, please send me an email so I can help you directly.

My email: Tom@InsurgentPublishing.com.

Good luck and keep creating.

Tom Morkes

Founder and CEO of Insurgent Publishing

PHASE 1

FUEL

Milestone 1: Understand Collaboration

Milestone 2: Develop the Collaboration Mindset

Milestone 3: Define What You Want

Milestone 4: Define What You Offer

Milestone purpose

To explain what collaboration means from a practical standpoint, how it works, and common obstacles that can hold you back from doing your best work.

Milestone checklist

- ☐ Define collaboration
- ☐ Overcome common negative myths of collaboration
- ☐ Understand the solution to these myths and how to apply collaboration to your project

MILESTONE 1

UNDERSTAND COLLABORATION

Do any of these problems sound familiar?

1. You've put a lot of time and effort into your business, but you're still not making the money you know you're worth
2. You've had some early success, but the wins have dried up and now you don't know what to do
3. You've tried every trick in the book, but you just can't seem to break through your current plateau

If you've ever experienced these problems, you're not alone. These are common pains that just about every entrepreneur faces at one time or another. The problem is, these pains compound when you work alone. Pretty soon, they become insurmountable.

While it's impossible to remove all uncertainty, risk, and the chance of failure associated with entrepreneurship, there are ways to limit downside while increasing your chances of success. This book will show you how.

Finding a better way

In 2012, Jon Nastor came up with an idea for a new business. Of course, like most ideas, he didn't know how feasible it was to build, let alone whether he could make it profitable. Regardless, Jon wrote the idea on a piece of paper. In total, it took eight lines of text to describe the product. This was enough to get started. This is when the first obstacle appeared: the idea was software based and Jon had no experience as an engineer or programmer. This was followed closely by the second obstacle: software usually requires an injection of capital to get started. Undaunted, Jon decided to move forward with the idea the only way he knew how: by collaborating.

Fast forward two years and Jon is the cofounder of Velocitypage.com, a 6-figure and growing company that he works on part time. He's also a collaborator on several other businesses and runs several podcasts, including the award winning *Hack the Entrepreneur*. Jon now has the freedom to pursue his favorite hobbies, start new business ventures, and spend more time with his family.

Jon's story is not unique.

Kira Slye is the cofounder of PolymerClayTV, a website devoted to the art of—you guessed it—polymer clay. For eight years Kira worked on this project part time, with little to no progress, barely making enough money to continue producing her podcast (Polymer Clay Podcast). It wasn't until Kira teamed up with her partner and took a different approach to their business, rapidly testing a new product idea in their market, that things changed. In just 50 days they sold over 500 spots to their $99 event. Kira and her co-founder are now looking for ways to grow their business, something that wouldn't have been possible had they not chosen to collaborate in the first place.

And there are plenty more examples just like Kira and Jon that we'll cover in this book, including:

- ✓ How Corbett Barr collaboratively launched a 6-figure membership site from scratch
- ✓ How Guy Vincent is collaboratively developing a tech startup with a remote team from all around the world
- ✓ How Chris Guillebeau started one of the world's most successful, fastest growing annual conferences by leaning into the skills of other people who had experience in this area
- ✓ How Danny Iny used collaboration to start his 7-figure business and how he pivoted early to find the right partner
- ✓ Why a relatively successful solopreneur switched to collaboration even though he was having great success by himself
- ✓ How a Captain in the Air Force collaborates in high-pressure, life-and-death situations (and what we can learn from this for our online business projects)
- ✓ And many more case studies

We'll also be covering topics in and around how to communicate and build a digital product remotely, how to coordinate and rapidly build a sales funnel, and how to launch your product before you ever build it by leveraging strategies, techniques, and procedures used by United States Air Force Intelligence Officers, Software as a Service product creators, fortune 500 consultants and more.

But before we get to the specifics, it's important to understand how we'll approach this topic.

Collaboration defined

If you seek out the definition of collaboration in a dictionary, you'll most likely find something like:

1. *A joint effort to achieve a common goal, or*
2. *The process of coming together to achieve something important more easily than can be done as individuals*

Both of these definitions are true in a literal sense, but successful collaboration is much more than this. For the purposes of this book, we'll further define collaboration as:

Two or more people working together:

1. *in a committed way with the intent of giving their absolute best;*
2. *in order to create something remarkable for their customers;*
3. *who do so by making the most of what each individual and the team as a whole has to offer;*
4. *who become even better collaborators for current and future projects as a result;*
5. *and who do all of this faster, more easily, and with greater financial return than they could on their own.*

This definition will guide the process I'll walk you through in this book. But for now, let's start with debunking some common myths about online business, digital products, collaboration as a whole.

Debunking myths about collaboration

Every person, regardless of circumstance, is capable of generating incredible results through the power of collaboration. Yet several insidious myths of collaboration continue to persist even in this age of connection, and unless we address them, they will cripple your project.

Myth #1. "I don't have enough time"

In 2014, I spent approximately 80 hours of time, spread across two months, building and launching a business incubator program from scratch. The program consisted of a seven day, in-person retreat at a resort destination in North Carolina. There were dozens of moving parts, but by collaborating with two others, I was able to focus on my strengths (marketing and sales funnel development), while my collaborators focused on other essential pieces (like the ecommerce solution to accept money payments, in-person event coordination, timeline development, etc.). This resulted in over $40,000 in revenue by the time we stopped taking new applications.

Later in 2014, I lead a collaborative project in a different niche. This one consisted of a six month mentorship and business training program specifically for veterans, which included the development of a comprehensive online training platform and private forum. Once again, I focused on the marketing and sales funnel development, and by the time we closed the shopping cart, we had raised over $20,000 in revenue. This took me about four weeks to build.

6 months later we launched a version 2.0 of the program. This time we generated over $25,000 in revenue in about a quarter of the time. After expenses and splitting the proceeds, both projects resulted in a healthy 5-figures per person.

We are now preparing a third launch and expect similar, if not better, results, with much less time and effort now that the systems and framework are in place.

Do you think you can spare 50-100 hours this year to work on a collaborative project if you were to generate 5-figures from your effort?

Myth #2. "I don't have enough money"

Every collaborative project I've worked on has been bootstrapped with minimal initial investment (less than $1,000). Many of the costs were further reduced because of the assets each collaborator brought to the table, whether previously built websites to host our sales page, or an ecommerce solution to take payments, etc. Beyond costs like web hosting and other necessities for a digital product launch, the majority of the investment was time, not money.

That's the beauty of collaboration—you don't necessarily need a loan or investment to get your project off the ground. The old adage "you need money to make money" might have been true 50 years ago when producers and consumers were quite disparate. Now, in the 21st century, where everyone has the means of production at their fingertips, and production is quite cheap, especially in the digital space (which we are focusing on in this book), nothing could be further from the truth.

Matt Helbig, is the founder of Valid 8, a service that helps you find collaborators, perfect ideas, and get your idea funded with equity-based crowdfunding. Naturally, Matt hears about new product ideas everyday. Through his platform, he helps people through the process of building their products, and realizes how much freedom collaboration can give to entrepreneurs who are starting from nothing:

"Traditionally, 50 years ago, if you had an idea for a business, you were going to go to a bank and you were going to write a business plan...and they'd give you money [which you're obligated to pay back]. Then, you go out and hire the services that you need. That's just a really limited way of doing things and it's extremely restrictive. Now, with the internet and social media...things have changed. This sounds contrived, but it changes a lot of things. One of the things that it has changed is collaboration, because even five to six years ago if you wanted to start a startup in Silicon Valley and raise money... it was like the old model, but pressed on to this new digital generation. But I think we're finding that startups don't need money [anymore]. What they need are services, and you can trade equity for services instead of trading equity for money to buy services. It seems logical to me. For example, the jet engine was invented after the reciprocating engine. Jet engines are extremely simple and reciprocating engines are extremely complicated. To me this is the simplest way of doing things and it just didn't exist before now."

How would your life change if you were able to replace your day job income from part time projects that require only a minimal investment of startup capital?

Myth #3. "I don't have an audience or connections"

I started from nothing. No connections, no audience, no platform. I worked as a solopreneur for more than 12 months trying to get traction (i.e. to get people to take notice of my work and buy my products). I made little progress and ended up in the red even though my overhead was low (I was doing all the work myself, afterall).

It wasn't until I started connecting and working with others that my platform and revenue took off. Collaborating allowed me to expand my network almost overnight. For example, by teaming up with John Lee Dumas and Antonio Centeno on HighSpeedElite.com, I was able to leverage the platforms they had already built to build our new collaborative business. This meant we had immediate access to potential customers right from the start. Further, by working with some of the best people in their respective industries, I was able to get my foot in the door with people in my own niche (publishing) simply by association. Let's be honest, Tom on his own is a nobody, but Tom working alongside [place name of important person here] makes a difference.

An important point to make here is that the above example of collaboration couldn't have happened without my involvement. Both Antonio and John were busy running 6 and 7 figure businesses--they simply didn't have the bandwidth to start a new veteran-focused business on their own. I say this to point out that collaborating isn't about riding somebody's coattails, but leveraging one another's strengths to their max. In this way, even if you start from nothing—no audience, connection or platform—you can still launch a successful product or business by collaborating.

How would your business improve if you were able to get access to the audiences of the biggest names in your industry?

Finding your collaborative edge

There are many ways to collaborate. The intent of this book is not to show you all the possible ways to collaborate, but instead to focus on a very specific style of collaboration that will dramatically improve your chances of online business success. The key criteria for this type of collaboration are speed, profit, and enjoyment.

#1. Speed

By default, I will show you the fastest way to get from point A to point B.

This is not the best practice for every collaborative project. Some collaborations benefit from a longer, more structured process, with multiple levels of accountability and validation (biotech research, for example). However, in the case of digital product launches for small businesses, speed is your friend. Time destroys profit and motivation. Your goal should be to move as quickly and efficiently as possible to achieve your goals.

#2. Profit

Not all profit is created equal. Scoring a $100,000 contract might seem appealing, but what if it takes you $95,000 and 12 months to deliver on that contract? Not so appealing any more, is it?

A healthier way to view profit is as a factor of net margin and opportunity cost.

Net margin is a measure of profitability, "which shows how much of each dollar earned by the company is translated into profits." —Investopedia.com[1]

Mathematically, net margin looks like this:

Net Margin = (revenue - expenses)/revenue)

Using the example above, if you bring in $100,000 in revenue, but it cost $95,000 to create, package, market, and sell your product, your net margin is 5%.

($100-$95)/$100 = .05 (5%)

That doesn't leave much margin for error, does it?

Companies like Walmart can get by on these type of paper-thin margins because of volume (lots and lots of transactions happening every day). For those of us with more limited resources, it's generally a better idea to focus on products and services with a higher net margin (which requires less volume).

As you can see, there are two ways to improve your net margin—increase the price of the good or service you're selling, or decrease the costs associated with selling said good or service. By creating and selling digital products, you can do both (which we'll cover in this book).

Opportunity cost refers to "the benefits you could have received by taking an alternative action."

To better understand this, ask yourself: *"what potential positive results are you missing out on from other projects you could be working on because of the work you're doing on your current project?"*

Speed and effort are essential ingredients here. The longer it takes you to produce the results you're going for, the more value is being lost from other projects you could have started, finished, and shipped instead. This is why it is essential to be able to deliver high margin projects fast, while investing the minimal amount of resources to achieve your goals (while still over-delivering and delighting your customers, of course). Anything more is waste, anything less and people will notice (and not buy).

When it comes to collaborating, it is best to keep overhead to a minimum while focusing your efforts on simple products or services that you can create fast and sell for a high price point. Hence, the preference for digital products when and where possible.

Note: the systems and processes you'll learn in this book can be applied to physical products and services, but for the sake of consistency, we'll focus on digital products.

#3. Enjoyment

Profit is not everything.

What is the point of collaborating if you're miserable throughout the process? What's the point if it means you lose out on more time with your friends and family? What's the point if you just don't care about the work you're doing?

No, enjoyment isn't everything, but your feelings toward the work you're doing, and with whom you're doing it, will impact your speed, energy, and excitement, which fundamentally alters the end result.

Further, the more enjoyable the working process, the more likely you are to stick it out through tough times (and there *will* be tough times).

When in doubt, I will focus on the most enjoyable ways to collaborate with others; this includes setting up certain systems and processes to encourage personal growth, team camaraderie, and a genuinely fun working relationship amongst collaborators.

Azimuth Check

When two or more people work together in a committed way to produce a remarkable product faster, with more ease and more financial return—this is collaboration. Collaboration will allow you to avoid many of the common problems faced by solopreneurs. It's important to realize that the time, money, and connections you already have are enough for you to begin collaborating, no matter what situation you're in. And from here, you'll be in a better position to launch your product, as collaboration can increase the speed of production, generate better revenue, and make the entire experience more enjoyable.

Take a short break here to take notes and collect your thoughts below before moving on to the next Milestone:

Milestone purpose

Develop the right mindset and beliefs to succeed as a collaborator.

Milestone checklist

- ☐ Understand mindset and belief and how they relate to collaboration
- ☐ Overcome common limiting beliefs about business and collaboration
- ☐ Implement the "Collaboration Mindset" into your life and work

MILESTONE 2

DEVELOP THE COLLABORATION MINDSET

Imagine this experiment: you put 100 entrepreneurs with nearly identical capabilities into a room, train them in the same critical business skills, and then give them all the same resources they need to be successful. What would happen?

According to statistics compiled by Harvard Business Review, here's what would happen:

Out of 100 entrepreneurs starting a new business venture, 25% would fail within the first year. Of the remaining 75 businesses, 36% will fail year two. Of the businesses that make it to year three, 44% will fail. And if you somehow make it to year four, there is a whopping 50% attrition rate.[1]

Of the 100 entrepreneurs who started, only 13 remain four years down the line.

So what separates the successful 13% from the unsuccessful 87%?

The difference between success and failure

First and foremost, some amount of luck plays a part. Some entrepreneurs get lucky; they land a lucrative contract out of the gate, they connect with just the right mentors to lead them through a sticky situation, they create a product which solves a problem that is just starting to get major press, etc.

But, while this concept of success being predicated upon luck (a concept popularized by *Malcolm Gladwell in Outliers*) has hints of truth, there's a single element that runs throughout every "lucky break" story, case study, or example. That is, the person who got the lucky break had to *choose* to take action in the first place. And he or she had to continually make choices throughout the process, with most of these choices made with limited knowledge, amongst infinite variables, in the center of uncertainty.

This, of course, is the nature of entrepreneurship: it is uncertain.

So the question becomes: what is it that motivates, cajoles, or instigates such bold action?

Perspective, belief, and actions

It is natural to look at the world and to think everyone sees what you see. We rely on this expectation to function in society. I would imagine no one would ever drive a car if they didn't expect other drivers would see them on the road. Shift the context from physical space to something less tangible, like ideas, and things change dramatically.

Take the case of politics; a single statement from a politician can be shown to a group of people and lead to applause or scorn. The exact same words, two entirely different experiences, two entirely different reactions. The difference? Perception and belief.

Perception is the world around you as you see it. Belief is the truth you hold about what you're perceiving. Your reality is a combination of perception and belief. In this context, your reality is almost certainly different than the reality of the person next to you (to varying degrees). This is why two people can see the exact same words and draw opposite conclusions.

We can begin to see just how important perception and belief is in our lives when we consider their ramifications—the choices we make and the actions we take. For example, your belief about the importance of some event around you will influence your choices and therefore your actions around said event. These actions produce results. These results then influence your original perception of the problem, usually (but not always) reinforcing your original belief. The inverse is also true: what you deem trivial will most likely lead to inaction, which will produce limited or no results, which will reinforce your original belief: that this particular event or thing *is* trivial. In either case, you have proven yourself right.

Apply this to business and it's understandable why some people seize opportunity after opportunity and create great results, while others who are working on the exact same problem, under similar circumstances, seem to struggle indefinitely and make little or no progress.

The difference?

One person has inculcated a particular belief system that aids him in pursuit of his goals (succeeding in business, for example), while another is floundering because of a set of limiting beliefs that are holding him back from achieving his goals.

How to overcome the most common limiting beliefs about business and collaboration

I've seen hundreds of solopreneurs fail—I've even been one myself. As is naturally the case, with every failure comes an excuse. Because of my work as a consultant, mentor, and coach, I've had the opportunity to hear just about every excuse in the book for why people fail. Many of these failures could have been avoided by connecting and working with others, but their limiting belief pattern (like my own) kept them from collaborating.

The following are the most common limiting beliefs I've encountered around the topic of collaboration and why many solopreneurs choose not to collaborate (or attempt to collaborate but fail). For each limiting belief, I'll give you a way to reframe the concept to make the belief empowering (i.e. useful to you as an entrepreneur, business owner, and collaborator).

Limiting belief #1. Everything must be perfect before I launch. Good enough is not good enough. To ensure quality, I must have command and control over every element of the product creation and delivery...

Reality: Believe it or not, good enough is good enough. Perfection in business is a myth. Further, human beings value anything they personally create more so than had someone else created it. This is what Marketing Professor Daniel Monchon calls the Ikea Effect.[2] In reality, your best work probably isn't the best work *possible*. More likely than not, there is someone better skilled than you who can do better work than you in a particular area of your business. If you can find this person and work with him or her, the entire project will be better off for it.

Limiting belief #2. The world is a zero-sum game. There are winners and losers and there's no such thing as a win-win situation. If I take on a partner (or partners), then they're simply taking a cut of all my hard work...

Reality: Business is more like an ever-expanding fountain of wealth than a closed vault. The more value you create, the more value you capture. And there is no limit to the value you can create in this world, which means there is no end to the value you can capture, either. Therefore, the more great people you can assemble to work with you on your project, the greater the value you'll be able to create. As a result, everyone's piece of the pie actually becomes bigger, not smaller.

Limiting belief #3. Work is a struggle. Nothing comes easy...

Reality: Do about 10 minutes of research on the most successful business people on the planet and you'll notice some similarities. The most striking is this: none of them are busy. There is truth in the fact that many of them have probably worked hard for years, and the compound effect of their efforts have made things that much easier for them now, but that doesn't contradict the fact that it is quite possible to do less and enjoy better results. The fast-track path to this reality? Finding and leveraging a team of experts, so you can focus on what you enjoy and what comes naturally, while your collaborators work on the things they enjoy and come naturally to them. The most amazing things happen when your weaknesses are someone else's strengths, and vice-versa. What happens next is less effort and better results for all parties involved, including your happy customers.

Limiting belief #4. Work must be time-consuming. If I am not busy at all times, I am not really working and I have not earned my success (and therefore do not deserve it)...

Reality: There is no correlation between time and money. The most financially successful people in the world spend much less time working than the average blue collar factory worker. On the topic of "earning" success, answer this question: who earns the title belt more, the fighter who goes 12 rounds and takes a beating, barely coming away with the win, or the fighter who knocks out his opponent in the first 30 seconds of the first round, barely breaking a sweat? I don't know about you, but if I'm stepping into the ring, I'd rather be the latter over the former any day of the week.

Limiting belief #5. I work better alone. Teammates will slow me down and strangle my creativity...

Reality: You are not actually as good as you think you are, and if you believe you are that much better than others, that's hubris talking, not reality. The best fighters have a coach, the best writers an editor, and the best entrepreneurs have a collaborator to bring their results to the next level. Even the most iconic individual business leaders of the past century were nothing without the collaborators they worked beside: Bill Gates and Paul Allen, Steve Jobs and Steve Wozniak, Larry Page and Sergey Brin.

No one person can do it alone. The sooner you recognize this, the sooner you can start doing great work.

Limiting belief #6. Teammates, partners, or collaborators will take advantage of my time, effort, and intellectual property...

Reality: Most people team up to work on projects because they want something better than what they're capable of creating on their own. Conflicts may happen—we are all humans, after all—but this can be mitigated with an articulated vision, clear expectations, and a working agreement developed at the start (which we'll talk about later in the book).

A better question for you might be: how much time and effort are you wasting, and how many great things are you not producing, because you're not working collaboratively with others?

The collaboration mindset

The collaboration mindset is a way of thinking about business (and other collaborative projects) as win-win scenarios; where faster, easier, and more enjoyable work creates better results for ourselves and our customers than laborious, isolated, difficult work; that success correlates not with hard work, but with *great* work; that we are better off working together than alone; and finally, that every person is capable of collaborating.

Developing the collaboration mindset means adjusting your beliefs, including:

1. Beliefs about the power of collaboration
2. Beliefs about your role as a collaborator
3. Beliefs about the intentions and abilities of others

Consider the following examples of positive belief systems about collaboration in the table below. How would these change the way you approach business and collaboration?

Beliefs about the power of collaboration	Beliefs about your role as a collaborator	Beliefs about the intentions and abilities of others
Collaboration is good for you, your partners, and your customers—a triple win Better results come from better collaboration Successful collaboration comes from making the most of what is present and what is possible in the direction of accelerated achievement Synergy is the by-product of great collaboration Good collaboration is the fastest and easiest way to succeed. Period.	I can add real value to the collaboration and the collaborative process I am a good collaborator or can learn to be I can help draw out the collaborative capacities of others I can do and be my best for the good of the whole I can support the success of the project and each team member	Our team has huge potential individually and collectively People want to do their best to ensure our project succeeds—they are well-intentioned in their behavior People are willing to collaborate for the good of the whole Regardless of any immediate issues, a good solution can always be found People are willing to learn and grow to help us succeed

This is not an exhaustive list, but a primer to get you started. You may already be thinking about what you would add to the list, or how you might change it using your language—that's a good thing. Continue to add to this list. Even better, write them down on a notecard and tape it to your desk or workspace so you can look at these beliefs and reinforce them every day.

Reframing limiting beliefs into the collaboration mindset

Remember Steve from the beginning of the story? He struggled to find success from the outset. Let's evaluate his actions by observing the belief pattern *behind* his choices, compared to how Steve could have done more had he developed the collaboration mindset.

	Steve's limiting belief	**Steve's new collaboration mindset**
Belief construct	"I have to prove myself and succeed on my own first before I can get others on board."	"I can grow my business more quickly and easily by getting others involved from the start."
Belief influences thinking	"I will need to put in some serious hours to make sure I succeed, but once I am successful others will want to work with me."	"I can approach the right people to help me succeed—right now."
Thinking influences action	Steve willingly puts in exceptional hours and does all work on his own because he has to work hard and make something worthwhile first to be successful.	Steve approaches the right people and starts to build relationships that will support his long-term success, and he does this easily and rapidly.
Action influences results	Steve achieves a certain level of progress and success but it is taking much longer than he had hoped. He experiences extreme fatigue and his relationships with his family and friends are damaged. He notices how difficult the journey is.	Steve's decision starts to have a collective impact in terms of the quality of his partnerships, alliances, start-up team—his actions are amplified through working well with others. He notices how enjoyable the journey is and how easily it seems to be coming together.
Results confirm beliefs	Steve hasn't yet proven to himself that he is a success. Because of this, he keeps working alone until he can prove his worth. As a result, new relationships do not develop, doors do not open, and he is right where he started. He has proven to himself that his belief is correct.	His business begins to grow more quickly and easily and he starts to find bigger and better opportunities. He can leave his job before being laid off, and now his work is enjoyable and he has time for himself and his family. He's proven to himself that his belief is correct.

Lawrence Green on starting with mindset

Lawrence Green is a leadership and business consultant. Since 1996, he has worked with hundreds of teams of all sizes to improve their collaborative performance. Green emphasizes the importance of starting with mindset if you want any chance of success with collaboration:

"Great collaboration starts in the mind, with an intent to be a great collaborator, first and foremost, before someone actually develops the skills of being a great collaborator. So if someone's not sold on the value of collaboration, or someone doesn't really get the value of it, or doesn't see the need to be a great collaborator, that's going to get in the way of the process and could lead to failure down the road."

Collaboration mindset exercise

Now onto an important question:

If you accept that what you believe about collaboration matters, what would be useful for you to believe in order to be successful as a collaborator?

As a practice exercise, fill in the following chart to get clarity on your belief patterns and how you would like to view collaboration:

	The power of collaboration	**Your role as a collaborator**	**The intentions and abilities of others**
What beliefs would you like to hold strongly in each area?			

What would happen if you acted as if these beliefs were true?			
What is the first small step you can take, this week, to turn your intention into action?			

Azimuth Check

The biggest difference between success and failure is choosing to go forward and take actions towards your goal. These bold moves are motivated by your perception and beliefs. You must remember that good enough IS good enough. Business can be an ever expanding fountain of wealth, and you do not need to struggle or let work consume all of your time. It's important to evaluate your beliefs about collaboration and recognize that no one person can do it alone.

Take a short break here to take notes and collect your thoughts below before moving onto the next Milestone:

Milestone purpose

To help you approach collaboration in a manner that is consistent with who you are and what matters most in your life.

Milestone checklist

- ☐ Discover what makes you tick
- ☐ Define your definition of success
- ☐ Determine the ideal lifestyle you want to live

MILESTONE 3

DEFINE WHAT YOU WANT

A collaborative project is only as good as the collaborators who participate. But in order to choose the right people for the project, you need to know where you stand. Entrepreneurs who fail to do a self-examination are essentially flying blind. How do you know what to build, how to build it, or whom to work with if you don't know what you're after, in business and life?

If you want to make good choices in a business collaboration, you must be clear about who you are, what you want, and what you offer.

Unfortunately, a common mistake made by aspiring entrepreneurs is rushing into a project (collaborative or otherwise) without having done their homework. The homework, in this case, is conducting introspective analysis so you can know exactly who you are, what you want, and how you should approach collaboration, business, and success in general.

The following Milestones will walk you through a series of questions to help you gain personal clarity so you have a better chance of success in your collaboration.

Step 1. Start with why

The leadership expert, world renowned speaker, and author Simon Sinek, explains in his book, *Start with Why,* that great companies are the result of great leaders who start with a strong, intrinsic *why*. From this why stems the *what* and then the *how* of the businesses they build.

Before you dive into a collaborative project, you need to discover your why. Answer the following questions to gain clarity on your why:

Focus	Questions	Answer
Your personal why	What is it that makes you tick? What is your reason for being?	
	What do you want for yourself, your family, and the world?	
	What impact do you want to make in this lifetime?	

A strong why is the foundational element of every successful business. Before you begin collaborating, make sure you know your why. Once you know your why, make sure the mission and purpose of whatever project you intend to undertake aligns with these same values. Failing to find this alignment will lead to discontent, mismanagement, and, ultimately, regret.

Realizing you're not living your "why"

AJ Leon, founder of Misfit Inc. didn't think about his *why* until he had nearly reached the top of his financial career ladder.

"And on December 31, 2007, I was invited into my boss's office. I go in and sit down and he looks me in the face and tells me that I am getting a promotion and that I am going to be a junior partner in the firm. And I just let that soak in. That was a big moment for me. That was everything that you think you are supposed to work towards. And I just walked out of his office, down the hall, back into my own and I started to cry. I closed the door behind me and I just started to cry because I realized that I was trapped; I would never, ever, ever be able to walk away from that type of money. Any idea, and any thought that I ever had of living a life of meaning, and of purpose and of adventure was gone....

That was probably the most vacant moment of my life. I had never felt more empty than that and I just sat there and wept for 20 minutes. And then it just kind of occurred to me: you always have a choice, you could walk out right here and right now and you could leave everything you have ever known, and everything you have ever worked for behind; you could start again. And that's what I did.

I realized I was at that crossroads. So I grabbed my shit, put it in a box, walked into my boss's office, and he got the tail end of the Shakespearean soliloquy about the system, and then I took the elevator 28 stories down. For the first time in my adult life, I was free.

So, that was how I left my former life. But I didn't leave to start something. I didn't leave with this idea of Misfit Incorporated like many of my friends who were entrepreneurs; I left because I was evacuating a life plan gone horribly wrong.

So, through that process of leaving I just tried to reinvent my life from scratch—reinvent everything.

Who am I? What do I love? What do I actually love to do? Why am I here? Who are my friends? All of these things, through a cathartic thought process and a lot of writing I did over 18 months led me to developing this little project called Misfit Incorporated, which today is not so little anymore."

Step 2. Define personal success

If you don't know where you're going, any road will get you there. The same is true of any goal. How can you hope to achieve success (that elusive, ephemeral thing) if you can't clearly define and measure it?

First, be wary of defining success based on someone else's worldview. It is remarkable the number of entrepreneurs who define success purely in terms of dollar figures; specifically, dollar figures relative to peers, coworkers, or friends. This definition of success leads directly to the rat-race (competing against others for money, keeping up with the Jones', etc.).

If you don't take the time to consciously identify what success means to you, it is easy to find yourself living somebody else's journey. This usually corresponds with that nagging feeling that something in your life is missing. And it is. What's missing is you taking responsibility, ownership, and direction over your life and business.

Consider these questions to discover what success means to you:

Focus	Questions	Answer
Personal success	If you think about what you have achieved in your life so far, which achievements are you most proud of? Why?	
	What does this tell you about what you value most in your life?	
	If you could get to the end of your life and leave a legacy, what kind of legacy would you like to leave?	
	Who do you most want to leave that legacy for and why?	

Step 3. Define your ideal lifestyle

What is more important to you: $1 million in the bank, or living in a small beach town, in the house of your dreams, with a beautiful family, that you only need to work a few hours a day to support?

When it comes to an ideal future, a lot of people start with a grandiose number in their head, something like breaking 6-figures or hitting the $1 million mark, as if this number will change everything (or anything). It makes sense: these are cultural financial milestones that let you say to the world "look at me, I've made it."

But what if you didn't have to hit some arbitrary number to live your perfect life? What if you didn't need to slave away for years saving hundreds of thousands of dollars before you could switch to more rewarding work? What if only $5,000 per month—a number completely attainable by anyone willing to put in the work—gave you the freedom and security you needed to do what you love while providing for yourself and your family?

These are the exact questions I asked myself before I started down my entrepreneurial journey. Growing up below the poverty line, I always loved the thought of being financially secure. Naturally, I felt reaching that million dollar milestone would give me and my family all the security in the world. As I've gotten older, though, I've realized this million dollar milestone is a façade. Hitting a million dollars often comes with equivalent expenses that keep even millionaires teetering on the edge of bankruptcy. That's why my mind has shifted to a more practical view of finances and success, namely: passive cashflow (total number of zeros coming into my bank account every month without me doing anything).

Over the past several years, using the strategies outlined in this book, I've developed a few businesses that bring in several thousand in income every month, that is not directly correlated to the number of hours I work on them. This combined with other streams of passive income generated from various projects, and I have more than enough money to travel around the world with my wife, indefinitely. I'm also free to pursue whatever collaborative projects I want—things that can really impact the people who matter to me—as well as the ability to work on my own terms, including, but not limited to, when and where I work, how long I spend on which projects I choose, etc. For me, this is my ideal lifestyle. It may, and probably will, change in the future. The point isn't the particular lifestyle, but taking the time to understand how you work best and what you ultimately want out of the collaboration.

Before you commit to a collaborative project, make sure it fits your ideal lifestyle. Here are some questions that can help you discover your ideal lifestyle:

Focus	Questions	Answer
Ideal lifestyle	How much money do I need every month to sustain my ideal lifestyle?	
	What type of projects do I want to be involved in? Are there specific criteria these projects must meet for me to remain positive, energized, and motivated?	
	In what capacity do I want to work? Do I prefer working with others in person? Do I prefer daily or weekly live calls? Or do I prefer to work asymmetrically, working different hours than my collaborative partners and working those hours when and how I want?	
	If you were to create a picture of your perfect future, what would it look like? What adjustments could you make to that picture so that it is even more compelling for you as an attractive destination?	
	If your business was the perfect vehicle for helping you achieve success in your life, what would you focus on? What would you deliver and how would you run it so that it better served your life and vision for success?	

Azimuth Check

The foundation of your business will be understanding your *why*. Knowing the motivation and purpose behind what you do will serve as a constant source of energy for your work. Just as important, you need to understand your personal measures of success so you can work more clearly toward your goals. Following this path will allow you to make your ideal lifestyle a reality.

Take a short break here to take notes and collect your thoughts below before moving onto the next Milestone:

Milestone purpose

To help you define and clarify what you bring to the collaborative project.

Milestone checklist

- ☐ Define and understand your unique value
- ☐ Understand how you are different than others and why it matters
- ☐ Define where your unique value can provide the most value to other collaborators

MILESTONE 4

DEFINE WHAT YOU OFFER

Every collaborator brings both personal strengths and weaknesses to the table. Having a clear understanding of what these are will help you play to your strengths and avoid activities where you are weak. It will also improve your chances of success by making it easier to find the right people for your collaboration (i.e. experts with complementary skillsets to you). That's why you must be clear on what you bring to the particular project, to your partners, and to the business in general before you start assembling your team or building the product. This is where the Personal Inventory Assessment comes in.

The Personal Inventory Assessment is a framework for conducting productive self-reflection in relation to the collaborative project you want to start (or join). The Personal Inventory Assessment will force you to take a hard look at your strengths, weaknesses, passion, and purpose, which will help you make rational and wise choices.

Take your time on this Milestone and don't rush; you'll save yourself a lot of time, trouble, and potential stress by completing these exercises before you move to the next milestone.

Step 1. Define your superpower

What skills or activities come naturally to you, that others struggle with and would pay you for?

A superpower is any skill that brings value to your project, comes naturally to you (or is relatively effortless), and that others struggle with. Your superpower may include (but is not limited to):

1. Programming
2. Sales
3. Copywriting
4. Product development
5. Project management
6. Connecting / building relationships
7. Design
8. Leadership

Every person has (or can develop) a superpower. It doesn't have to be technical. Just because you can't code doesn't mean you can't work with coders to build a product. If you don't feel confident in any of the superpowers listed, remember that skills take time to develop. It's less important that you have a superpower right now than you're willing to develop one over time.

Here are a few questions that will help you discover and develop your superpower:

Focus	Questions	Answer
Your super-power	What comes naturally to you? What activities feel effortless? What do you do every day that other people find difficult?	
	What do you do that people rave about?	
	What do you do well that other people pay money to have done for them?	

When effortlessness and value don't collide

Just because you can shotgun a Mountain Dew in 2.5 seconds, or you can reach level 1,000 in World of Warcraft doesn't mean these skills are superpowers. A superpower must be applicable to the project at hand, so if you're working on a pop-chugging startup or a WOW startup, these skills might help and therefore might be considered superpowers. In every other case, they are not.

The point is this: superpowers must be relevant to the business or project you're undertaking. Which leads us to Step 2: Quantify Your Value.

Step 2. Quantify your value

What value does your superpower bring to others?

Once you identify activities that come naturally to you, you must determine the value they bring to (1) your project and (2) your potential customers and clients.

Here are a few questions that will help you determine the value of your superpower:

Focus	Questions	Answer
Quantify your value	How does your superpower add value to your clients or customers?	
	What do you bring that will uniquely enrich the collaboration project?	
	What is your greatest talent or strength that will help your project to succeed?	
	What are the other strengths and skills that you have that will add value to the project?	

You want tangible, quantifiable metrics to properly measure your superpower. Be specific and be realistic; exaggerating a superpower does a disservice to yourself and to whatever collaborative business you undertake (sooner or later the rest of the group will find out and the entire project could fail because of this).

Understanding where you add the greatest value

Chris Ducker, founder of VirtualStaffFinder.com, manages multiple companies and hundreds of employees, and facilitates the preparation of thousands of virtual assistants' bios and resumes for potential employers. Needless to say, Ducker has a versatile set of skills and knows how to multitask. However, he is not successful because of his ability to multitask, but because of his ability to focus on what he is great at and outsource or delegate the rest:

"In the beginning of 2008, I launched my current group of companies, which are still operating. There are three subsidiaries and we have almost 300 employees. This is what I do. I mean, I am the author of 'Virtual Freedom,' I'm a blogger, a podcaster, and a speaker and all that stuff, as well...but at the very core of everything, I am a sales and marketing guy and I don't lose sight of that."

Ducker understands that his greatest superpower is being able to market and sell products and services. By knowing this and fully embracing this, he's able to delegate all other tasks to people who are much stronger than him in other areas. For example, while he might be a great manager (and surely he must be to operate multiple businesses with over 300 employees), it's important to recognize that Ducker does not consider management his superpower, and therefore he does not spend his time managing, but has instead surrounded himself with others who are more capable than him in those tasks so he can focus on marketing and sales.

Step 3. Identify your weaknesses

In what activities do you struggle?

A chain is only as strong as the weakest link. So too, every team is only as strong as the weakest team members—or rather: the weakest *activity* of a team member. For example, if you're working with an engineer and a marketer on a new digital product, but you have the engineer working on sales and marketing and the person with years of marketing experience coding the program, your collaboration will have a greater chance of failure than had you placed each individual where they are best suited—to their particular superpower.

Identifying your weaknesses is important because then you can find a collaborator who is strong in that area to replace you. In doing so, you can mitigate many of the perils of a new business venture and increase your chances of success moving forward.

As you go through this section, know that this is not a time for bravado or pride. You do not serve others, or yourself, when you ignore your personal weaknesses or pretend they don't exist. Use the following questions as an opportunity for learning and growth that will ultimately make you a better person, collaborator, and leader.

Questions that will help you discover your weaknesses:

Focus	Questions	Answer
Weakness discovery	What do you struggle with that other people find easy?	
	What irritates you to the point of frustration?	
	What activity would you rather pay to have done for you rather than attempt to do yourself?	
	What particular weaknesses do you need to make sure you manage for the good of the project?	

Why you need to identify your weaknesses

An honest reflection of your own weaknesses serves two purposes:

First, by reflecting on your weaknesses, you know what you can (and may want to) improve. At the end of the day, you're responsible for your own success—no one else. Therefore, it's best you develop the mindset of constant improvement and progress. However, we can only improve that which we are aware of—so taking personal inventory of your weaknesses is the starting place of growth.

Second, by reflecting on your weaknesses, specifically in relation to your superpowers, you can know who you should or should NOT approach for a joint venture or collaborative business.

For example, if you hate sales and your palms get sweaty when someone brings up money, you should look into finding someone proficient at sales and marketing. Conversely, you should avoid teaming up with someone with the same fears—it wouldn't serve you or the project to do so. Or let's say you're great at connecting and selling. If this is the case, perhaps you should find someone who can manage and run the backend of your project, so you can focus on these higher value, complimentary activities.

A strong collaboration includes team members with complementary but different skillsets. Therefore, you can only choose the right collaborator by knowing your personal superpowers as well as your weaknesses.

Understanding Your Weaknesses in the Context of Collaboration

Sean Ogle is the founder of Location 180, a website devoted to helping entrepreneurs develop location independent businesses so they can live and work anywhere in the world. Ogle practices what he preaches and has built Location 180 into a sustainable and thriving business while traveling around the world. However, building his platform to what it is today required more than just the skillsets he brought to the table. On a number of occasions, he's had to team up with others to build and launch various digital products. Here's Ogle on what he looks for in a collaborator, specifically in the context of understanding his own weaknesses:

"When I am looking for people to work with, I am looking for people that have complementary skill sets to me. Not the same skillset, but people that are going to bring something to the table that I can't do. This means you need to understand your own personal strengths before you reach out to connect with others. Coding or design are great examples of complementary skillsets in my case because I am not a coder or designer. Another example might be project management; when it comes down to all of the details—making sure everything is done on time, making sure that everything is organized—I am terrible at that. So when I am looking to work with someone, I want to make sure that they have got one of those skill sets, because otherwise I could do it myself; the marketing stuff, I can do all of the front facing copywriting, or blogging, or product creation. I want to make sure that if I am going to give someone equity in the business or if I am going to work with them, they are bringing things to the table that I personally cannot do."

Step 4. Determine your working style

What is your preferred way to work? Do you like rigid guidelines or are you comfortable with ambiguity? Are you task oriented or are you relationship focused?

There's no right or wrong answer to your preferred working style, but it is important to understand how you approach both work and collaboration so you can choose the right teammates for a project. When you know your preferred working style, and the preferred working style of your collaborators, you are less likely to miscommunicate, disagree on the execution of the project, or do double work.

Take a moment to fill in this quick exercise to better understand your own working style. You will use this chart in conjunction with finding your ideal collaborator in Milestone 6:

<table>
<tr><th colspan="8">Dimension 1: Task vs. relationship</th></tr>
<tr><td colspan="4">I tend to emphasize task completion over team relationships.</td><td colspan="4">I tend to emphasize team relationships over task completion.</td></tr>
<tr><td>1</td><td>2</td><td>3</td><td colspan="2">4</td><td>5</td><td>6</td><td>7</td></tr>
</table>

Dimension 2: Preference for structure						
I prefer to approach goal achievement in a relatively unstructured manner.				I prefer to approach goal achievement in a highly structured manner.		
1	2	3	4	5	6	7
Dimension 3: Level of detail						
I am more of a visionary, big picture type of thinker.				I am more of an high detail type of thinker—I want to understand all the details.		
1	2	3	4	5	6	7
Dimension 4: Perfectionism vs. pragmatism						
I want my work to be absolutely perfect before putting it out into the world.				I prefer to do the best I can with the time I have and then put it out into the world.		
1	2	3	4	5	6	7

Understanding your results

Task vs. relationship

When working on a project, do you emphasize task completion or relationships? If you overemphasize task completion, you risk undermining the quality of relationships necessary for an effective collaboration; and if you overemphasize relationship harmony at the expense of task completion, you will take too long to the finish and ship.

An ideal collaboration involves a balance of both.

Preference for structure

Every entrepreneur has a preference for structure; some prefer more (clear path with milestones, timelines, and specific actions to take on a daily basis), some prefer less (working through uncertainty, executing rapidly, and doing whatever it takes to reach your goal). Do you resonate more with the former or the latter?

Whichever type of structure you prefer, it's important to know that others may fall along different ends of the spectrum, so you must be able to work with both types of people.

Level of detail

Do you prefer big-picture thinking or are you a task-oriented person who enjoys executing specific, clear objectives? The level of detail you prefer will impact how you work given various tasks and is an indicator of who you should surround yourself with. For example, big-picture thinkers should work with task-oriented collaborators, and vice-versa. A team of big-picture thinkers will make execution more difficult, and if all collaborators are task-oriented, it's possible to lose site of the scope and purpose of the project, and how everything ties together, from marketing and sales to product creation.

Perfectionism vs. pragmatism

The perfectionist wants everything to be perfect before they release something into the world. This may mean they do not ship very often. Pragmatists, on the other hand, ship relentlessly, ignoring imperfections, sometimes to the detriment of the project.

Being an extreme perfectionist or pragmatist could sabotage your collaborative effort, the former by slowing progress to a crawl (when speed is of the essence), the latter by shipping poor work (thus damaging your relationship with your customers).

The ideal collaboration includes individuals who balance both perfectionism and pragmatism. In the event that you lean toward one extreme or the other, look to find collaborators who can balance you out by being the opposite.

Guy Vincent on why knowing your working style is paramount

"If you have a team that is motivated and you trust them, then working remotely is totally fine."

Vincent elaborates on what it takes to make remote, collaborative work a success:

"It's important to be clear on what you want to do, and it's better to make a decision on something that you feel needs to be done for the company, rather than being stuck in this kind of perpetual limbo of not making a decision."

Just because Vincent takes the lead as the CEO of Publishizer, he always takes advice from his collaborators and makes sure to consider the pros and cons of every recommendation given to him from his team:

"If you're constantly pulled in many different directions it's easy to get stuck inside your head, but you have to bring it back to:

What are our strengths as a group, right now?

What can we achieve now that will have the most impact towards what we want to achieve (which, in our case, is user growth, sales through the platform, and customer happiness)?"

Azimuth Check

In order to successfully collaborate, you need to be aware of your strengths and weaknesses, and find people with complementary skill-sets to your own. By using The Personal Inventory Assessment, you'll be able to recognize your superpower and the value it brings your potential collaborators and customers. You'll also understand the areas where you are weaker, which will help you to determine the type of collaborator with whom you should work. Determining the set of skills that would be most helpful in a potential collaborator is crucial, but it's also important to think about how your work styles mesh. Having a collaborator with complementary but different skills to you will allow you both to conquer the areas of your project in which you excel.

To get acess to a bonus resources and digital templates from this Milestone, go to: www.tommorkes.com/collaborate

Take a short break here to take notes and collect your thoughts below before moving onto the next Milestone:

PHASE 2

ASSEMBLE

Milestone 5: Develop Your Profitable Idea

Milestone 6: Define Your Ideal Collaborator

Milestone 7: Build Your Team

Milestone purpose

How to create a well-defined, viable business idea to take to your potential collaborators.

Milestone checklist

- [ ] Brainstorm possible potential products or services
- [ ] Use the Profitable Idea Framework to mitigate the downside risk of choosing an unprofitable idea
- [ ] Conduct your idea summary and decide on what idea you plan to move forward with

MILESTONE 5

DEVELOP YOUR PROFITABLE IDEA

Developing a profitable idea isn't just necessary for your personal success—it's essential for getting any type of market leader to consider collaborating with you. People are busy. The last thing you want to do is approach a potential collaborative partner with an incomplete idea. Therefore, before you start approaching potential partners, you need to clarify and refine your idea. To do this, we'll brainstorm a list of potential ideas, run them through the Profitable Idea Framework filter, and then summarize the best ideas to so they're presentable to potential collaborators.

Idea generation 101

"You've got to remember that 99% of the time nobody wants [your idea]. Most offers that appear to an entrepreneur as a good idea are actually horrible, horrible ideas."—Eric Ries, bestselling author of *The Lean Startup*[1]

When you begin brainstorming, remember: quantity is better than quality. Many of your initial ideas will be unrealistic, vague, or otherwise unusable. Therefore, the more ideas you can generate, the greater the likelihood that one of them will be a profitable venture. Further, by focusing on quantity, you avoid narrowing your thinking too soon and missing out on alternative, potentially more lucrative, ideas.

Let's get to it.

Step 1: Brainstorm problems

In order to find your profitable idea, you need to get all of your ideas out of your head and onto paper (or a computer screen). In the following space, write down all the problems you deal with on a daily basis. Consider putting yourself in the shoes of others and brainstorming a list of problems that others go through as well. Be specific and go for quantity over quality:

Step 2: Brainstorm solutions

Take the list above and describe possible solutions to each of these problems. Again, quantity is more important than quality at this point:

Step 3: Prioritize your list

Take your list of problems and solutions and go through them one by one, listing them in order of most interesting to you personally.

Step 4: Choose your top 3 ideas for further analysis

Identify your top three solutions and list them below. These will be the ideas you put through The Profitable Idea Framework.

1. ______________________________

2. ______________________________

3. ______________________________

The Profitable Idea Framework

The purpose of The Profitable Idea Framework is to save you time, money, and energy by filtering out potentially unprofitable ideas so you can focus on an idea or course of action with the best chance of success. Not only will this framework give you a cohesive, developed idea to share with potential collaborators, it will give you personal clarity over the project (something you won't get from keeping the idea in your head).

The Profitable Idea Framework will help you better define and refine the problem, solution, customer, market, and competition, as well as help you estimate the profitability of your idea so you can make an informed decision on whether to proceed.

The Profitable Idea Framework			
Focus	**Question**	**Yes/ no?**	**Proof/comment**
The pain	Does your customer have a distinct problem or pain that needs fixing?		
Awareness	Is your customer aware of this problem?		
Desire	Is your customer actively seeking a solution?		

Solution desperation	Does this problem cause enough pain / frustration in the customer's life to warrant a change (either by purchasing a solution or from switching from their current solution to yours)?		
Customer purchasing power	Does your ideal customer have the means to afford your solution?		
Distribution	Are you able to reach your customer directly?		
Competition	Are there at least 3 competitors in your space?		
Cost	Are you capable of producing a solution with your own funds (i.e. without outside investment, loans, etc.)?		
Profitability	Can you sell your solution above the cost it takes to create and deliver your solution?		

Calculate potential upside

How much will you need to spend to enter this market and provide a solution? Can you realistically make a profit based on this investment?

When you consider profitability, you don't need extensive spreadsheets or advanced calculus to run the numbers (at least not at this stage). Instead, you need to look at four things:

1. Current Problem Cost: What is the cost, to your customer, of their current problem?
2. Current Solution Price: What is your customer paying to solve this problem right now?

3. New Solution Production Cost Pricing: What will it cost you to produce and deliver a better solution than what is currently available?
4. Upside: Can you provide a better solution at a lower cost to an expensive problem your customer is currently dealing with?

Here are a few examples based on real businesses (note: this is third party analysis done by me, and may or may not be something these businesses considered before they started):

Idea	**Current problem cost**	**Current solution price**	**New solution production cost and pricing**	**Upside**
WP Curve (a WordPress support company)	WordPress support is confusing, difficult to manage, and expensive. Downtime on a website can cost hundreds or thousands of dollars.	1. Do it yourself (cost: time) 2. Outsource (cost: $50 - $1,000+ depending on fix needed)	By leveraging inexpensive but skilled workers, WP Curve can offer WordPress support at a fraction of the cost of freelance or consulting work.	Significant
High Speed Elite (a business mastermind + mentorship program for veterans)	Veterans want to start businesses, but don't have the experience or support to get their businesses off the ground. This lack of experience and mentorship could cost tens or hundreds of thousands over time.	To learn to build a business, most veterans can: 1. Do it yourself (self-taught; could take years) 2. 2+ years and $100k+ for an MBA	Small group coaching and mentorship from 6 and 7-figure veteran business owners, delivered via live webinars and FB forum (very little overhead).	Significant

Velocity Page (a WordPress plugin that lets you edit any page directly without going into the backend of WordPress)	Any person who uses WordPress knows that editing pages can be a long, painful process because the page editor is slow and difficult to master.	There is no real solution for this, except for switching to a new platform (cost: high), or choosing a new theme (cost: high, depending on how much work needs to be put into modifying the new theme to make it work).	It's difficult to gauge how long or how expensive it will be to develop software, but since there are over one million WordPress users, it seems there would be a lot of growth potential for a plugin.	Medium to high

If the current problem cost is high, and the current solution price is high, and you're capable of solving the problem better than the current solution at a fraction of the cost, then you have the foundation of a profitable idea. Anything else should be considered unprofitable unless you can prove profitability. For now, sideline these alternative ideas (you can always come back to them in the future).

Go ahead and fill out your information in the chart below:

Idea	**Current problem cost**	**Current solution price**	**New solution production cost and pricing**	**Upside**

Once you've crossed off the non-profitable ideas, it's time to build your idea into a proper business model for testing, measuring, and validation

Make the stop/go decision

Should you proceed?

At this point, some opportunities will seem better than others. That's a good thing—it means you've started to refine your idea into something more tangible, which we'll develop into a full plan in the next Milestone. Now consider one final set of questions before deciding which option should be pursued, reworked, or abandoned completely:

If greater than 50% of your answers to "The Profitable Idea Framework" are a definitive "no," scrap the idea. If 75% or more of your answers are a definitive "yes," it's a good indicator you're on the right track. For those ideas that fall in between, more research must be done to make the stop/go decision. Consider reevaluating these ideas until they're better developed and you can answer "yes" to more of the criteria above.

Remember, it is better to make the stop/go decision now than to invest time and money, hoping somehow things will work (they won't).

If you decide to "go" it's time to take the next step.

Conduct your idea summary

Once you decide on the idea you want to move forward with, it's time to summarize what you know. The answers you place in the summary table below will help you to articulate (to yourself and others) what your project is about and why it is worth building. This will make it easier for potential collaborators to see the value of the project and for you to sell them on the value of being involved, which we'll cover in Milestone 6 and 7. In the meantime, fill out your Idea Summary chart below:

Type	Question	Answer
Problem summary	What problem are you solving?	
Solution summary	How will you solve the problem?	
Customer summary	Who is your target audience / ideal customer?	
Competitor summary	Who are the competitors in your space?	
Cost	How much will it cost to create your solution?	
Pricing	How will you price your solution?	
Distribution	How will you reach your customers?	

From ideation to action with Chris Guillebeau

Chris Guillebeau, bestselling author of *The $100 Startup*, founder of The World Domination Summit (an annual conference that draws more than 3,000 people every year), and blogger at chrisguillebeau.com warns against staying in the idea stage too long. Guillebeau says it's important to generate and develop your idea into a clear vision, but it's equally important to move forward with it:

"The next step is to explore and to have conversations...but there is one specific thing that I do see happen a lot of times with aspiring entrepreneurs: people have an idea, this burgeoning idea, and they don't really know where it is going to go. That is fine, because that happens to everybody with every project. [The problem is] they start talking to people about it and they never really make progress."

Guillebeau summarizes his point as follows:

"Conversations are helpful, but for something you really want to develop, it really has to move to action at some point. The sooner the better, in my opinion."

Moving forward

At this point, you have completed your Personal Inventory Assessment and you have put your brainstorming through the Profitable Idea Framework. This should help you to feel more confident in your abilities, desires, and goals. You also have the prerequisite information outlined so that you can find the right collaborators to work with. You know what strengths will complement your weaknesses and vice versa, and you can more clearly communicate to potential collaborators the product you will be building. In the next Milestone, we're going to identify the specific type of collaborator you should find, connect, and work with for your project.

Azimuth Check

Before you approach a potential collaborator, you need to have a fully developed idea. By using The Profitable Idea Framework and The Idea Summary framework, you'll have a more fully-developed idea. Once you can clearly see and articulate the potential upside to your project, you can move forward.

Take a short break here to take notes and collect your thoughts below before moving onto the next Milestone:

Milestone purpose

To understand exactly who you should work with to help make your collaboration a success.

Milestone checklist

- ☐ Understand the characteristics of an effective collaborator
- ☐ Define your ideal collaborator
- ☐ Use the Portfolio Metric to refine your search

MILESTONE 6

DEFINE YOUR IDEAL COLLABORATOR

Who do you need on your team to bring your idea to life?

This should be the primary question you ask yourself as you conduct research into potential collaborators for your business project. In order to determine who you should connect with to collaborate, you need to understand what makes a great collaborator. In the following section, I'll walk you through the characteristics of an effective collaborator as well as provide a framework to vet potential collaborators (which we'll do in Milestone 7). Let's get to it:

Characteristics of an effective collaborator

#1. Hustle

Hustle is the ability to work toward the completion of a goal even if there is little to no supervision or direction, or if the path is uncertain.

For a lean, fast-paced collaborative project to work, every collaborator must have hustle. If even one person in a small group waits for instructions or can't deal with uncertainty, the entire project could collapse.

Questions you might consider here in helping you to define your ideal collaborator:

Focus	Questions	Answer
Hustle	Do they have a fundamental hunger for learning and success?	
	Are they willing to take charge and run with a task even if they are not clear at the start exactly how they are going to do it?	
	Is this person a creative problem solver? Is he or she capable of taking an idea and running with it, even if the path is uncertain?	
	Are they self-directed and capable of working autonomously?	

#2. Follow-through

Follow-through is the ability to take a task to it's final stage and to ship it to market. If, for example, the task is adding a new feature to your software, someone with follow-through will complete the code and get it up and running and operational with minimal guidance, instruction, or supervision. He won't wait to hear "go" from someone else (unless that was specifically discussed beforehand). Someone with follow-through will also follow up on incomplete tasks even if they aren't the task owner (we'll cover the particulars of this type of collaborative work in Milestone 9).

While hustle is essential, *follow-through* ultimately makes the hustle worthwhile.

After all, a collaborator might have great ideas, he might even be able to put in the sweat equity (read: hard work) to begin turning these ideas into reality, but is he capable of hitting publish? Can he or she see the task all the way to the finish line? A common stumbling block for collaborative projects is one or more collaborators lacking confidence to complete and ship, which can lead to a string of unfinished tasks. This can cripple your project. Make sure you choose someone who is capable and confident in taking a task to it's final iteration and who is comfortable shipping complete work.

Questions you might consider here in helping you to define your ideal collaborator:

Focus	Questions	Answer
Follow through	Does this person finish what they start?	
	Do they have a track record of completed projects?	
	What do previous collaborators say about their work and ability to finish and ship projects on time?	

#3. Integrity

Bottom line: you should never do business with someone who lacks integrity. He or she might be capable in every other area, but if they lack integrity, the entire project can become compromised. Of course, you could mitigate this risk by creating a very detailed contract, but even then you're giving up part of the joy of collaboration, which comes from having faith in your business partners as you both work toward a common goal.

The best way to determine someone's integrity is to seek out dishonesty in their prior business projects. Ask his prior partners—did he pay on time? Was he transparent with his reports? Did you have a good experience? Unless you ask these hard questions, you'll have no idea who you're dealing with.

Note: this isn't to scare you away from collaboration, but to give you the awareness to mitigate risk. Make sure you do your due diligence as best as possible when you research potential collaborators, and always be as specific as possible in terms of standards (we'll cover this later in this Milestone).

Questions to consider before you choose a collaborator:

Focus	Questions	Answer
Integrity	Does this person have a transparent online persona and use their real names for projects?	
	What do their prior partners or collaborators say about them?	
	Have they had any financial troubles previously? How have they handled this or other potentially negative scenarios?	

#4. Collaboration mindset

You can't be a great collaborator if you don't fundamentally see the value in collaboration. Collaboration only works if both parties approach the collaboration from the same positive mindset; that collaboration can make us better, help us build a better product, and allow us to work more easily and rewardingly by letting us focus on our greatest strengths.

Anyone who needs to be convinced of the collaboration may not be a good fit.

The following questions will make sure your potential collaborator values collaboration the same way you do:

Focus	Questions	Answer
Mindset	Does this person see the value in collaboration?	
	Have they been part of a collaboration before? What did their peers and collaborators think of their collaborative effort?	
	If they are inexperienced with collaboration are they willing to learn?	
	Are they excited by the value of this project? Are your values and vision aligned?	

#5. Complementary but different skillsets

Finally, you need to find someone with a skillset that complements yours. The most effective collaborations are a combination of people who support one another by leveraging their own unique strengths.

For example, for a non-technical business founder, a complementary but different skillset is finding a technical cofounder, such as an engineer or programmer. Anyone looking to launch a software business would benefit from having someone invested in the project who understands the technical side of the business. As another example, for a creative project like publishing, this could mean finding people who are uniquely good at marketing and selling, and others who are good at writing engrossing fiction. The last thing you would need is a group of great writers if none of them have the skills to market and sell their books (or at the very least a desire to learn how).

Here are a few questions that will help you determine whether a collaborator's skillset is complementary but different enough for your project:

Focus	Questions	Answer
Skillsets	What are you building? Can this person help you build it faster or better than you're capable of doing on your own?	
	What key role will this person take? If you had to give him or her a title, what would it be?	
	What exact skills and abilities do you need on your dream team?	
	What skills and abilities will complement what you yourself bring to the project?	
	What can others bring that can help amplify your chances of success?	

What to avoid in a collaborator

A successful collaboration requires a dream team; that is, a small group of people who can add the most value to your project—who can bring it to life better than anyone else. **In this way, the worst collaborators are people who are just like you**. While it might be tempting to choose someone because they are similar to you in style, belief, and vision, this can be potentially destructive to the project. If your collaborator doesn't provide a unique voice—if he or she simply echoes your ideas—what is the point of collaborating in the first place?

Similarly, you should avoid building a team of friends. While this might make you feel comfortable, it can also make it difficult to have hard conversations, which, when not confronted, can paralyse a project. The fine line here is if your friends also happen to have complementary but different skillsets that add clear value to the project. In either case, make sure you don't jump into the project blindly. Follow the process outlined in this Milestone and in Milestone 7 to make sure that, if you choose to work with a friend or family, they are chosen because they are the perfect fit for the project.

The Portfolio Metric

There's no 100% certifiable way to determine whether a potential collaborator has the traits listed above, save for actually working with them. Of course, the nature of the type of collaboration we're talking about doesn't lend itself to this type of experimental discovery—it would take too long and a bad fit could result in a failed project.

The good news is, there is one heuristic in particular that can tell you a great deal about a person and give you a good sense of whether they'll be a good collaborator. This heuristic is called The Portfolio Metric.

The Portfolio Metric can be administered by asking the following questions about a potential collaborator:

1. How many projects has this person shipped in the past year? In the past decade?
2. How do peers describe him or her? How about past collaborative partners?
3. What do customers say about his / her work?

The more transparent a person's portfolio of work, and the more public the work they do, the more you can trust this metric to tell you whether they'd be an acceptable collaborator.

What The Portfolio Metric can't tell you is whether you should not work with someone. That is ultimately a choice you have to make based on your best judgement, after you've gone through the evaluation process in this Milestone. At a minimum, I recommend not working with anyone who doesn't have a clear track record of success (not financially, but based on the character traits listed earlier).

Use the following chart with all prospective collaborators:

The Portfolio Metric	
Questions	**Answer**
How many projects has this person shipped in the past year? In the past decade?	
How do peers describe him or her? How about past collaborative partners?	
What do customers say about his / her work?	

Why you should focus on the best in the world

When I say best in the world, I'm referring to the people who are regarded as the best in their industry, by people in their industry (the word "world" is very micro in this sense). I will refer to the best in the world interchangeably with "expert"—both refer to someone at the top of their game.

The reason you want to focus on the best in the world is for the same reason you should be collaborating in the first place—to improve the product or service you're building, and to increase your reach, impact, and sales at the same time. The best in the world (aka industry leading experts, leaders, and linchpins), generally have access to two things that can dramatically improve your chances of success: expert skills and a vast network.

Jon Nastor and working with the best in the world

Remember Jon Nastor, the ex-punk rocker turned serial entrepreneur, from the beginning of the book? When Nastor first had the idea for

Velocitypage.com, he knew he needed a skilled programmer to build the WordPress plugin. One way to find a skilled programmer is to use a platform like upwork.com (an online database of freelancers). For the right price, you can find quality programmers who should be able to handle the job.

The problem with this approach is that it's time consuming and expensive to find the right programmer. Additionally, someone for hire does not have the same level of skin in the game that you have. If things don't work out, the freelance programmer still gets paid and can move on to the next client. You, on the other hand, have much more at stake...

Instead of hiring a team of programmers, Nastor went the collaborative route. While most people interested in collaboration would start looking for potential partners amongst friends and connections, Nastor did the opposite—he looked outside his immediate connections and focused on who in the WordPress community could deliver amazing results. It didn't take him long to find Mark Jacquith, a lead developer of the WordPress platform itself.

There are thousands of WordPress developers in the world, but Nastor chose Mark for a few reasons. First, it gave Velocitypage.com instant credibility. People knew Mark and trusted the projects he worked on. It also gave Velocitypage.com immediate access to their ideal customer (WordPress users). How much faster could you become a profitable business if you had instant access to a group of customers who were ready to buy?

Nastor never considered going to anyone other than the best in the world for help. He did this for two primary reasons. The first and most obvious reason: if you're going to turn your idea into a reality and produce your best possible work, you're going to need the best possible people to make it happen. The second and less obvious reason is this: there was a higher likelihood that no one had asked this person to collaborate because of their perceived status in their niche or industry.

Here's how Nastor summarizes the fear many solopreneurs have when it comes to approaching the best in the world to collaborate:

"For instance, [no one has asked] to do a partnership with [Jacquith] because everybody's afraid. Because, well, he's a top guy, you don't ask him, right? If I'm just a nobody in the WordPress market—which, I was absolutely a nobody in the WordPress market—why would Jacquith work with me?

Honestly, this thought didn't even cross my mind, and I don't think it should cross anybody's mind [who is looking to collaborate]. Actually, I've never really thought about this until now. For me, it was more like 'obviously he's going to do it with me, because it's a good idea.'"

Why the first collaborator is paramount

While it's important to do your homework about any person with whom you collaborate, the first collaborator is most critical. There are two primary reasons for this:

First and foremost, the first collaborator is the person closest to the genesis of the idea. At this point, you should have a rough draft of your idea (your idea summary) and a clear understanding of your goals, desires, strengths, and weaknesses. While the business model allows you to take practical action, it's still just an idea, and ideas are fragile. Choosing the wrong person with whom to collaborate could lead to slow progress (when speed is essential), moving off course (when focus is key), and early team conflict (when teamwork is crucial).

Second, the first collaborator helps set the culture. A single person by himself has character. Two or more people working together on a project have culture. That culture is a reflection of how your team interacts, both in a work capacity and outside the office hours. By selecting the right collaborator, one with the right characteristics, complementary but different skillsets, and aligned vision, you increase your chances for developing a valuable culture that can grow with you.

Why a successful solopreneur stopped going it alone

Dan Norris is the co-founder of WP Curve, bestselling author of *The 7 Day Startup*, and co-founder of Black Hops Brewing. In the past ten years, Norris has started multiple businesses, many of them as a solopreneur. It wasn't until recently that he gave up the solopreneur route to pursue collaborative business development. Here are the results in Norris' own words:

"For the first seven years of being an entrepreneur I worked for myself in a freelance type capacity. Now I am working on three different businesses with three different groups of people and it's a totally different experience.

One of those businesses is WP Curve, which I co-founded with Alex McClafferty. We are up to a team of 40 people now. We have been operating for 2.5 years and have thousands of customers customers and $80,000 in monthly recurring revenue.

I learned a bunch of things in my last business; one was that I didn't want to run a business by myself anymore because it was just too stressful. I knew I didn't have all the skills I needed to make it work. This was especially true with WP Curve, which is a 24/7 WordPress support company. It was going to be impossible for me to run that by myself. Plus, no one wants to be the sole point of contact for a business that runs 24 hours a day.

So, I was either going to employ people, or find a co-founder. I actually started WP Curve by myself and ran it for about a month or two that way. Then one day, I wrote a blog post on the WP Curve blog about my other company failing and this guy named Alex replied to the post and started talking to me. He had just moved to the United States and he was looking for something to do. He said that he would work for me for free. I told him I was looking for someone who could help with sales, as well as someone who could cover that side of the world, so it was a good fit.

After two months, it was clear that this thing was taking off. We had about 20 customers and a lot of potential. Since Alex and I were already in it together at this point, it was a no brainer to continue to collaborate with him and make him a co-founder. Some people probably think I am crazy for giving away half of my business to some guy I don't know, but I'd rather own half of something big, than 100% of something tiny. And we both wanted something big. And believe it or not, we actually worked together for over a year without ever meeting each other in person."

Azimuth Check

You learned earlier how important it is to find a collaborator with different but complementary skill sets. On top of this, your potential collaborator should be someone with hustle, follow-through, integrity, and who shares your positive mindset towards collaboration. The most reliable way to judge how they will be as a collaborator is to use The Portfolio Metric to determine their track record. Finally, when picking your collaborator, you want to team up with the best in the world—someone who knows what they are doing and has experience. Remember how important this first partner is going to be as you bring your idea to life in the coming Phases and Milestones.

Take a short break here to take notes and collect your thoughts below before moving onto the next Milestone:

Milestone purpose

To give you a clear path and framework for connecting with collaborators.

Milestone checklist

- ☐ Develop a list of potential collaborators
- ☐ Connect with your ideal collaborator
- ☐ Decide to move forward or keep looking

MILESTONE 7

BUILD YOUR TEAM

How do you find, connect, and enlist the help of the perfect teammate (or teammates) for your project?

This is the question we want to ask now and the focal point of Milestone 7.

If this question seems challenging, don't worry—by completing all the Milestones up until this section, convincing your ideal collaborator should simply be a matter of presenting material you've created in previous Milestones, specifically your Idea Summary from Milestone 5.

As far as finding and connecting with your ideal collaborator, in this Milestone I'll show you exactly how to find and engage with potential collaborators in a non-salesy, non-pushy way that inspires them to join your project, as well as how to deal with rejection if it happens (and it happens to the best of us, unfortunately).

Let's get to it:

How to find your ideal collaborator

Step 1. Define your market / industry

Reference The Idea Summary from Milestone 5: what market are you serving? What industry are you in? Sometimes the product you're trying to build will cross markets or industries—that's okay. Feel free to segment this list to get as specific as possible, as well as to define all the potential markets where your product belongs.

Step 2. Create a list of experts in your industry

Once you've defined and segmented your product by industry, it's time to look for the experts in these fields. These are often a select number of people who are constantly being referenced across your industry; these are the type of people who are considered experts or authorities in their field.

Name	Industry / market	Interests / goals	Contact information

Step 3. Determine your ideal collaborator's goals

Before you approach any person with a business idea, you need a clear vision of the project (which you should have from the previous steps), and a clear understanding of:

- ✓ The person you are contacting (background and skillsets)
- ✓ His or her desires (in business and life)
- ✓ Where exactly you fit in the equation (specifically addressing the skills you bring to the project in the frame of benefits to the collaborator)

Question 1. What does this expert want in business and life?

Want to work with an expert? You need to understand their platform and what they want. Chances are this person is not interested in a business idea that might end up being marginally successful. More than likely, they will want something that either helps them succeed financially (brand building, new revenue stream, etc.) or emotionally (an altruistic project that means something to them).

Questions worth answering:

Focus	Questions	Answer
Collaborator	Why does the project matter, financially or otherwise, to this person?	
	What's in it for the expert? Is this a lucrative project? Why is this worth their time versus all the other things they could be working on?	

By researching your prospective collaborator in conjunction with completing your Idea Summary from Milestone 5, you should be able to show a potential collaborator exactly what you offer and why it matters.

Question 2. Where do you add unique value to this project?

Why does this expert need you at all? What is stopping this person you're reaching out to from simply building the idea himself? Will you truly be a value-add to this person and to this project?

Questions to consider:

Focus	Questions	Answer
Your value-add	What do you bring to the table? What's your value-add? Why do they need your help?	
	What results can't they create without your help?	
	Why collaborate at all? What makes teaming up better than alternatives?	

How to reach out to experts

Step 1. Lead with value

It's easier than ever to connect with just about anyone on the planet. What seems like a unanimous blessing is really a double-edged sword. It's great because there is very little stopping you from connecting with people who could change your business and life in a very profound and positive way. It's dangerous because the ability to connect with others is so cheap and easy, too many entrepreneurs approach networking recklessly, thereby destroying any chance of building a real, lasting relationship. If you've ever gotten spam in your mailbox, email inbox, LinkedIn account, or via any other medium or platform, you know what I'm talking about.

To avoid the spam filter of busy experts, there is only one thing you can do: lead with value.

Nobody cares about your idea. But people do care about things that will improve their lives. By leading with value, what could potentially come across as a shameless pitch becomes a generous offer to help. Ways to lead with value include:

1. Let the person know you have shared or promoted their work with your audience (or intend to)
2. A specific offer to help with something this particular person would find valuable (refer to the discovery questions asked in the previous point)
3. Positioning your collaborative project in terms that are beneficial to them first and foremost

Value creation isn't rocket science, but it does take time and effort to develop the right type of relationships (and you must start by creating more value than you capture).

Make it selfless

"I want to know people. If I'm going to collaborate with people and work closely with them, I want to know who they are and what matters to them. My intent is that the project doesn't just deliver the result in terms of vision for the project, but that it really works for the people who are involved. So when I make that invitation, I'm not making it from the basis of 'oh I want to manipulate person X to behave in such-and-such a way.' Instead, I'm thinking, 'how can I make this project work for this person' and then I figure out a way to make an invitation that speaks to them."—Lawrence Green, founder of Leader Greatness

Step 2. Work your connections

In the world of business, there is nothing more powerful than an introduction. Successful people have filters. They almost unanimously block out anything that seems like spam (including an offer to work together). But an introduction from a trusted friend removes the spam filter. It allows them to take an honest look at what you're building. You should always prioritize a personal introduction over any other approach. This means you need to do some self-reflection and consider your current connections:

Focus	Questions	Answer
Connections	Who do you know?	
	Do any of these people have an extended network that might be useful for your project?	
	Can you make your offer short and sweet and position it in such a way that it's a win-win if your friend attempts to introduce you to a potential collaborator?	

The good news is that technology has made working your connections even easier

To begin, log into LinkedIn. In LinkedIn, you can see immediately who you're connected to, and if you search someone's name, you can see how many degrees of separation you are from them. If you know who you'd like to work with, but you don't have them in your immediate network, this is a great strategy.

Step 3. Make the invite

Making the right invitation is important so that you get a clear 'yes' or 'no' from people so that you don't lose momentum. You want to find the right potential collaborators and make it easy for them to be definitely 'in' or definitely 'out'.

Leverage multiple touch points

There are more ways than ever to connect with people and to stay in touch. You should not be averse to leveraging any platform that your ideal collaborator is using. Further, it generally helps to connect on multiple platforms so that the potential collaborator can't forget to respond. A single email can get lost in an inbox fairly easily. A direct message on Twitter, a follow up on LinkedIn, and a reminder email will be much harder to ignore (and thus, a response is more likely).

Here are a few of the platforms I recommend using to connect with your collaborator

Blog

If you're building a product that you want to launch online, chances are the experts you should focus on have a web presence, generally in the form of a website or blog. Most blogs are a great medium to engage with your ideal collaborator. First, because blogs are personal. You taking the time to read and respond to a blog post means a lot (few people recognize this, which puts you way ahead of the game when you do it). Second, blog posts are much less noisy than a person's inbox. If you want to get noticed, go where your ideal collaborator is located and where the least amount of people are vying for his attention. Most likely, that is his blog.

The best way to connect with your ideal collaborator on a blog is to leave a thoughtful message on several blog posts over the course of several weeks. You can compound this effect by sharing and promoting these blog posts, and making sure to tag the author in all your messages (so he knows you're sharing his work).

Email

Email is the best way to connect with an ideal collaborator about your idea. Emails are personal, and most experts read and respond to emails that lead with value. The best way to leverage email is to keep the first one short and sweet, focusing on the bottom line value the collaborator gets from working with you on this project. Provide as much detail as necessary to get the point across that you're serious. This ultimately requires your best guess on how much you should add or how simple you should make it.

Once the first email is sent, follow up on other touch points like Twitter and LinkedIn to let the collaborator know you just emailed him. This will ensure your email does not get lost in his inbox, and it gives you the right to now start a conversation on other platforms, which ultimately makes the other person feel more comfortable.

Cold email template:

"Hey [Name of Expert], just wanted to say I'm a really big fan of your work.

I've been reading your blog and listening to your podcast for years.

In your last blog post you mentioned you were really interested in [place description of topic here].

I'm working on a new project on [topic] that will [describe features / benefits in regard to users].

I believe this could be a very important, lucrative project. I'd love to borrow 15 minutes of your time to tell you more about it in detail to see if you're interested and how you can get involved (with minimal time investment but great upside).

Let me know a good time to talk.

Stay in touch.

- Your Name"

Twitter

From the outside, Twitter is a simple social media platform built around 140 character text messages. While it may not seem like enough space to really connect with people, there are hundreds of thousands of creatives and professionals who use Twitter. Further, once you connect with your ideal collaborate on Twitter (you follow them and they follow you back), it's very easy to Direct Message them about your idea. This is best done in conjunction with one or more of the other touch points mentioned in this list, and best used as a reminder to the person about a longer message you sent elsewhere.

Twitter outreach template:

Hey Name-of-person-here, sent you an email about Name-of-Topic a few days ago. Just checking to make sure you got it.

LinkedIn

LinkedIn is the social network for professionals. If you're connecting with an expert in your industry, there's a very high probability he or she has a LinkedIn profile (note: if they don't, this could be a concern and worth considering why they wouldn't). The best part about LinkedIn—you can see very easily exactly what this person has worked on and shipped. This is useful when considering the Portfolio Metric we discussed in the prior Milestone.

As a rule of thumb, do not use the LinkedIn email messenger application. There's not much more than spam in LinkedIn email messaging app, so it's not necessarily worth your time to draft and send something here. The best way to leverage LinkedIn is to add the person to your network after you've reached out via email, blog, and Twitter, and let the person know you did.

The following template will more than likely result in a confirmed connection, which you can then use to send follow up messages if you ever need to.

LinkedIn outreach template:

Hey Name-of-person, just wanted to connect on LinkedIn. I recently emailed you about a potential collaboration that I think would really benefit your platform without much work on your part, and would love to share more about it with you.

The most effective techniques for cold email outreach

Justin McGill, founder of LeadFuze, sends thousands of outbound emails everyday. Here's McGill's advice on how to make your cold email outreach most effective:

"Quick hitting emails always work best. Typically, anything over 5 sentences and you will see your response rates drop dramatically. Limit each email you send to **one** call to action. Don't ask them to visit a link, then provide feedback, then schedule a time to chat. Break these up over three different emails if need be. Do not go on and on about how great your solution is. Find that ONE pain point you help to solve and mention that briefly. Generally, stick with one sentence about you or your product. The rest should be focused on them (their pain points, what they've done, etc)."

McGill also reminds us of the importance of bringing the email back to the recipient:

"Stroke their ego first and foremost. Do not come in asking something of them. I recommend engaging with them in multiple ways first before trying to ask for something. For example, I use Twitter mobile notifications to alert me when certain people make a tweet. This way I can quickly favorite/retweet/comment on their post. I've done this for months at a time with editors at key publications (to land several big guest blog opportunities) and just to generally get influencers to know who I am."

Following up

What if they say no?

Sometimes people are busy. Sometimes visions don't align. Sometimes a project needs more time to incubate before it's ready for a collaborator. Whatever the case, just because an expert says no to working with you does not mean the project is worthless.

If you get the benefit of receiving feedback from a potential collaborator, definitely take their advice seriously. The project may be critically broken right now, or perhaps your presentation needs to be reworked. In either case, constructive criticism from a potential collaborator is useful.

Next step: go back to the drawing board to reevaluate and confirm your original business idea. If everything still feels right, reach out to new potential collaborators. Just because the first person said no does not mean someone else wouldn't love to be a part of what you're building.

What if they say yes?

At this point, it's time to have a talk about the scope of the project.

Plan for a 15 minute call with this person. For the first minute or so, just try to connect with this person as a human being. Use this time as an icebreaker to get comfortable with one another.

Once you've broken the ice, introduce your idea based on the Idea Summary you created in Milestone 5. Your pitch should only be a few minutes long, focusing on:

1. Overview of the project and why it matters
2. Features of the product and main benefit to the customer
3. What you bring to the table
4. What you see the other person bringing to the table (which is why you're contacting him or her in the first place)
5. Tentative timeline and goals

If this call goes fine and you find that your ideas resonate with this person, the next step is to agree upon the project scope of work, timeline, and standard operating procedures for how you intend to collaborate.

Finding a partner for Velocitypage.com

Earlier I explained how Jon Nastor knew he needed to go straight to the top when he found his first collaborator, Mark Jaquith. Nastor knew that Jaquith was one of the very top people at WordPress, but that did not stop him from sending out a cold email to him. He was confident in his business idea, and had defined Jaquith as the type of collaborator he needed to work with.

"So, I emailed him, and he completely ignored me. And FINE, I emailed him again about a week and a half or two weeks later, and then I do what I have now learned to do. I went on to Twitter—and I already followed him—and I just said, 'Mark, I dropped you an e-mail,' and he was like 'oh yes, totally!'

I saw on his blog that he said that he was terrible at email and stuff so that is fine. To me that is one big thing. If you email someone one time, because you really want something, and they don't answer, don't just think that they maybe read it and don't want to respond to you. People just get busy, things get missed all the time. I miss things in my inbox all of the time. Just email them again. If you annoy them and they actually do not want to respond to you, they will probably say 'sorry, no, not right now.' That is it, that is what people do. So Tweet at him.

He read the email, we jumped onto a phone call, and he liked the idea"—Jon Nastor

Azimuth Check

When you do go searching for the right collaborator, keep in mind your market and industry. As you know, you want to reach out to experts in their field. For each possible collaborator, think about their personal goals and desires. How would this project affect this individual? Why are you the person they should work with? When you reach out to them (through email, their blog, twitter, etc.) lead with value and confidence, and keep your message direct and personal.

Take a short break here to take notes and collect your thoughts below before moving onto the next Milestone:

PHASE 3

CREATE

Milestone 8: Set the Foundation for Collaborative Success

Milestone 9: Plan Your Project

Milestone 10: Develop Your Product

Milestone purpose

To start your collaboration in a manner that is most likely to help you and your team succeed.

Milestone checklist

- ☐ Establish your working agreement
- ☐ Establish roles, responsibilities, scope of work, and project parameters
- ☐ Mitigate early team risk through agreements and conflict resolution strategy development

MILESTONE 8

SET THE FOUNDATION FOR COLLABORATIVE SUCCESS

For a small team to operate effectively, communication is vital. For a small team in charge of deploying lethal force against enemy combatants from thousands of feet in the air, communication is life or death.

Captain Marc Aalderink is a United States Air Force Source Intelligence Analyst. At his last duty station, Captain Aalderink was assigned to a Remotely Piloted Aircraft unit (what the media often refers to as drones). The purpose of this RPA unit was to fly surveillance missions throughout Afghanistan. They were also called in to perform a number of search and destroy missions. As part of a three person crew, it was Captain Aalderink's job to make sure the flight crew received and distributed the right information at the right time. This meant he had to be in constant communication with not only his own crew, but those in charge of the Operational Environment in which they flew, friendly forces on the ground, higher headquarters, and more.

As you can imagine, with so many points of communication, messages can get confusing, and important information could get lost. That is unless you have a system in place to receive, analyze, and share relevant information with your team, and a process in place for doing so in the right way at the right time.

Here's how Captain Aalderink explains the nature of RPA missions in a combat zone:

"One interesting thing about the way that a Remotely Piloted Aircraft operates is that it's nothing like it is in the movies or videogames where you see this clear-as-day picture, where the analyst is sitting back in Langley, saying 'okay I can tell by his retina scan that this guy is the bad guy.'

The image we work with is unclear. We call it a soda straw. At any given time we are looking at a very small piece of ground. And so, because we are halfway across the world while operating the RPA, we are very dependent on the people around us and other enterprises on ground to help get a full ground picture of what is going on. The guys on the ground are obviously going to have better situational awareness than us because they are there, they are seeing it with their own eyes. Then there are the imagery guys who are somewhere else and they are going to have a better idea of historical statistics (what has happened at a given location, at any given time) and how that applies to us on this current mission.

My position in all of this is to try to put it all together and package it up and help feed that system so it can accomplish the mission safely with no civilian casualties."

I asked Captain Aalderink about how, with so much input from so many people, he's able to decipher what's important to tell his air crew versus what's important to know, but not vital for the operation:

"If you see something wrong (or think you do), you need to speak your mind. You are not trying to cause confusion in the situation, but if you see something that you know is wrong, you have an obligation to bring it up, no matter who you are in the crew, whether you're an imagery guy, or whether you're a person on the ground providing intel. There might be 30 people actively supporting a mission like this and each person is critical. If someone sees something that could be off, they need to communicate it and try to be clear about it."

In a situation where two pieces of information conflict, like the location of an enemy combatant, Captain Aalderink had this to say:

"During a mission, you'll have many people call out what you are seeing on the ground. If they are not saying the same thing and if it is not sitting right with me (if it just doesn't seem right), I have to say something. Because it is a lot more damaging to strike something, hurt something, or even guide friendly forces to some place they shouldn't be, than it is to hold the trigger and go after the target another day."

Establishing your project standards

In order for collaboration to work, you need to set standards for your project. Your job as the leader of a collaborative project is to develop an environment and working relationship where collaborators work well together on product development, complete tasks on time and to standard, and are ready to launch by the ship date.

A few basic areas that you want to explore together are:

1. Purpose
2. Goals
3. Scope of Work
4. Roles and responsibilities
5. Project Parameters
6. Collaborative Assets

7. Agreements and contracts
8. Conflict resolution

The latter areas are particularly important to establish at the start because most people ignore these. Thinking there will never be conflict is a dangerous assumption. Even if people are passionately committed and agreed about the direction, there will still be differences of opinion about the best way to travel (ideate, create, launch, etc.).

The goal here is to reach agreement with your collaborators around how you want to approach the project itself. We will touch on each area in this Milestone.

Step 1. Define the project purpose

In the same way that we began during our self-analysis in Milestone 3, we want to begin our collaboration with a collaboration analysis. The purpose of your project is the glue that holds you and your collaborators together, and ties you each uniquely to the project.

The most useful purpose will be one that is ambitious, but realistic, and that the entire team believes in. It's also important to note that your project purpose can shift over time.

For example, with HighSpeedElite.com, our original purpose was to help veterans successfully transition into the civilian world. This is an ambitious, realistic purpose, and we all believed in it. However, after our first 5-figure product launch, we realized that not every veteran resonated with us, but only those who were interested in business. This is something that maybe should have been clear from the outset, but it's often difficult to know how to position yourself from a marketing standpoint when you're just starting out.

We've since shifted our purpose to helping veterans transition into successful entrepreneurs and business owners. When we launched the second iteration of our product, our messaging was much more refined and aligned with our purpose. In the end, our second launch did better financially because we were better able to find our ideal customers and deliver a message that resonated with them. This is why it's so important to establish your purpose at the outset, but also not be afraid to change it to better serve your customers.

Questions to discuss with collaborators:

Focus	Questions	Answer
Define your purpose	Why exactly are we here?	
	What is the dream?	
	What does success look like to us as a group? As individuals?	

Step 2. Define project goals

Every project needs a goal. A goal, unlike your purpose, must be measurable. For example, with HighSpeedElite.com, our purpose may be to help veterans transition into successful entrepreneurs and business owners, but our goal needs to include a metric to measure the success or failure of this purpose.

The best way to create a measurable goal is to use the traditional SMART framework:

1. Specific—How clear can you make your goal? How much can you niche it down to focus on one thing?
2. Measurable—What is the measuring stick you will use to determine success or failure?
3. Attainable—Is this within the bounds of reality for you to accomplish? Be realistic.

4. Relevant—Does this goal matter to all the collaborators involved in the project?
5. Time-bound—Have you set a date for completion of this project?

For example, with HighSpeedElite.com, our ultimate goal was to build out a full-featured business training platform that we could then scale to a broader audience. However, due to individual collaborators' prior commitments to their jobs, family, etc., this goal was not attainable. This meant we needed to define a smaller, more specific goal that would be a stepping stone to what we ultimately wanted to build.

We decided to focus on launching a small mentorship training program, which would allow us to work one on one with new students and build out a training platform with their direct input. Our metric for measuring success: new students. We put the number at 10 students as the internal success goal. We also said that less than 5 students would be considered a failure. This is an example of a very specific, measurable goal, that is relevant, time-bound, and attainable.

We ended up with 7 students. We didn't reach our internal goal, but it was enough to move forward building the program and platform.

Questions to discuss with collaborators:

Focus	Questions	Answer
Define project goals	What do we need to achieve in order to succeed?	
	How will we know when we have arrived?	
	What feels like a realistic timeframe?	
	What does success look like? What does failure look like?	

Step 3. Define the Scope of Work

If you've ever worked with a contractor, you've probably seen a Scope of Work (SOW). An SOW outlines the project deliverables and responsibilities. These generally include items the contractor is responsible for creating or delivering, in what format, medium, and condition, and based on a predefined timeline.

You want to create something similar for your project as soon as you can after a collaborator agrees to work with you on your project.

As a quick note: you don't want to treat the collaborator like a contractor. This would defeat the point of collaborating in the first place. Instead, the point of an SOW is that everyone is on the same wavelength. If a collaborator agrees to do art or writing for a project, but halfway through you expect them to do phone sales or pitch investors, you've done a disservice both to the collaborator and the project. While it is important that all collaborators remain flexible and willing to take on duties or tasks outside of what is originally established in the Scope of Work, you should aim to define key deliverables and expectations early on.

How Publishizer.com organized their collaborative scope of work

After Guy Vincent started the development of his book crowdfunding platform Publishizer.com, Vincent quickly brought others on board. His first collaborator was Martin, a developer living in Singapore.

In order to facilitate the remote development of a new crowdfunding platform, Guy wanted to make sure that the tasks of the project were clearly laid out before the project began. Luckily, Martin felt the same way:

"I was lucky in a sense that Martin is the most organized person in the universe, whereas I am not. So Martin brought to the table really clear documents based on how we were going to be working together. Originally, it was the scope of the project, what were the deliverables, what is the budget, how many hours were going to be required. He also used time tracking software in his regular client work, so I was able to go in and see how much time was being spent on what.

We used Trello which is a collaboration tool based around Kanban—cards with tasks moved along to the right until they are complete. So I could see what my collaborators were working on at any point in time. They could post comments or ask me if they required clarification. They told me what they required me to do, which was to provide wireframes.

One of the keys to us working successfully was a clearly defined scope of work. For example, engineers typically hate to be told to do design, or hate to be told to do sales or marketing. And of course, that's not their job. Either you have to do it, or you have to find someone who can do it for you.

Collaboration works best when you let people thrive on the work that they are great at. So I always let my collaborators work on what they thrive at."

Questions to discuss with collaborators:

Focus	Questions	Answer
Define the scope of work	What does our timeline look like?	
	What type of project do I want to be involved in? Are there specific criteria the project itself must meet for me to remain positive, energized, and motivated?	
	How will we work together?	
	How do we make sure that we make the most of our talents?	
	How do we make sure we are smart about execution?	
	How will important decisions be made?	
	How will we review our progress?	

Step 4. Define roles and responsibilities

First, let's start with some definitions:

1. A role is your primary position within a collaboration.
2. A responsibility is anything that has been assigned to you to complete and ship.

Every successful collaboration includes defined roles and responsibilities. To be clear, roles and responsibilities do not limit a project. While collaboration is a fluid, organic process in many situations, to build and launch a product requires every collaborator to be responsible for specific parts of the project. There are simply too many moving parts to hope that you and your collaborators will organically find out who needs to be doing what (this is a recipe for disaster).

Also worth noting, just because there are defined roles and responsibilities, this does not mean they are assigned *to* you. Because this is a collaboration, you want to determine individual roles and responsibilities as a collective whole. During the Collaboration Assessment discussion, each person has the opportunity to say what he or she is good at and where their talents would best be leveraged. This is an incredible opportunity to discuss what role you would like to take, and which particular tasks you'd like to be responsible for.

In general, every project requires someone to take the following roles:

#1. Lead Collaborator

The Lead Collaborator is the person leading the charge, and like a movie producer, is responsible for the whole production. The main responsibility of the Lead Collaborator is to make sure everything and everyone moves toward the shared goal, and that everything moves as smoothly as possible. The Lead Collaborator is also responsible for diffusing any conflicts, making sure everyone contributes, and is primarily responsible for project management (making sure timelines are hit and the project ships on time).

#2. Operations

This is the person responsible for most of the backend work, making sure pieces of the project are being developed, and taking a big part in the production of whatever needs to be produced. Whether your marketing plans include a podcast, blog, or technical engineering, the person in charge of operations would make sure the content is created on time and to standard. This is usually the role of the technical cofounder.

#3. Finances

This is the person responsible for the budget, keeping track of expenses, setting up payments, and doing the books. The person in charge of finances should also handle invoicing, payments received, and money distribution to collaborators.

#4. Marketing

This is the person in charge of marketing and sales initiatives.

Some examples of marketing initiatives include writing sales copy, creating social media content, developing or managing the development of graphics for sales and marketing purposes, and promoting the product and marketing campaigns (such as webinars, podcasts, blogs, etc.). This is by no means an exhaustive list of tasks, but should give you an idea of what you will be responsible for if you take this role.

Roles and responsibilities summary

Clearly, many parts of these roles will include shared responsibilities for tasks. And if you're only working with one other person, you'll each need to wear several hats (Lead and Marketing, for example).

Questions to discuss with collaborators:

Focus	Questions	Answer
Define roles and responsi-bilities	What are the roles for each team member?	
	What are the responsibilities of each team member at this time?	
	How do we make sure that the load is evenly shared / that everyone is contributing?	
	How will we keep our commit-ments to ourselves?	
	How will we revisit roles as the project evolves?	

Sean Ogle on defining roles at the outset

"It also really helps people really feel confident in those roles. So, if you have the one guy who is all about community, people know they can go to him, he knows that is his main role and he doesn't have to stress about making sales, or making sure the website is running properly or anything.

And so, I think that establishing those roles early on and even if that means everyone involved has a business background and they all can do each of those other things. Making sure that every person has their specific focus has been one of those key roles to success in any collaborative project that I have ever worked on."—Sean Ogle

Step 5. Define project parameters

Because I run a number of online, collaborative projects, I have to deal with multiple teams on a variety of tasks on a day-to-day basis. Because these teams are remote, the conventional approach to management (i.e. constant supervision) won't work. Instead, what I focus on is objective-based management.

Every collaborative project has an overarching goal, and the achievement of that goal is broken down into milestones and tasks. In order to manage and lead a remote team, you must focus on the individual milestones, ensuring that tasks are being completed on time and to standard.

The best way to facilitate this process is through the development of parameters.

A parameter is a set of guidelines that establish what we referred to in the Army as "left and right" limits (in other words, as long as you stay within these two lines, you're fine). Parameters let collaborators focus on intent rather than specific actions that must be taken in a given situation and allow for freedom, speed, and flexibility of action.

Examples of parameters

A few examples of parameters for your project might include the following:

#1. Quality over margin

If a decision must be made on which key features must be added to your product, the decision should be made based on quality even at the expense of margin.

#2. Relationships over sales

If you're working sales for your project, and the challenge you face is closing a deal fast versus building a relationship with the potential customer, you should default to relationship building, even if it means losing a sale.

#3. Learning over financial return

If you are in the early stages of getting your project up and running, and you have the opportunity to generate new streams of revenue, the deciding factor should be: does this contribute to learning and growth, and is it in alignment with the intent of the project? If not, scrap it and move on.

Questions to discuss with collaborators:

Focus	Questions	Answer
Define project parameters	What is our project edge?	
	What are our most important group values?	
	How should we work together? How should we work with customers?	
	If we want our team / project to be known for anything, what should it be?	

Step 6. Define assets brought to the table

One of the greatest benefits to a strong collaboration is the fact that collaborators often bring assets to the table. Assets can include:

1. Investment capital
2. A team of employees or VAs
3. Content that could be repurposed and reused

4. Tools and software that could help build or sell the product you're creating
5. Backend infrastructure (think website, ecommerce platform, etc.)

Whatever you and your collaborators are bringing to the table, it's important to talk through them and decide what can and will be used to develop your collaborative project.

As a quick warning: never assume anything. You may be collaborating with someone who has access to a massive audience, but they have no interest in promoting this collaborative project to their audience for a variety of reasons. The point isn't whether that's a good idea or not (you should have that discussion, though), but to make sure you understand going into the collaboration what you can expect from your teammates and what they can expect from you. While it might seem awkward to talk details like this early on, it will avoid grievances and conflict later on, so it's entirely necessary.

Questions to discuss with collaborators:

Focus	Questions	Answer
Define collaborative assets	Besides hustle, what are you bringing to the table? What are the other collaborators bringing to the table?	
	What would be valuable assets for this collaboration?	
	What are individuals willing to bring to the table? What assets are off limits?	
	Is everyone comfortable with these boundaries?	

Step 7. Define agreements and contracts

This is the part of the collaboration that most creatives (and even some business people) dread, but it's as important, if not more so, than all the other elements of successful collaboration. The reason is simple—agreements and contracts help to clarify both the project (including scope of work, goals, and objectives), as well as all participant roles. Some form of agreement or contract is essential if you want to make a collaborative project last. In the following section, I'll share a few examples of the various types of working arrangements you can set up.

Please understand—I'm not a lawyer so this isn't legal advice. You should consult an attorney if you intend to draft up some form of working agreement or contract for your project.

The handshake method

Let's be honest—not every project is big enough in scope to warrant a 50 page contract with multiple addendums. Perhaps you're working on a side project with a friend, someone you've known and trusted for years, and you want to try your hand at shipping something small on the side, like a free podcast or a free ebook. In this case—depending on your relationship with the collaborator—a handshake agreement could be enough to make sure you're both on the same wavelength about the project particulars.

When you should use a contract

Many people avoid contracts because it feels like an awkward conversation. The reality is that contracts, in the context of collaboration, aren't about holding someone culpable for errors if they happen, but to make sure everyone's clear on the project, the timeline, the goal, and responsibilities. Written contracts shouldn't be avoided. On the contrary, written contracts should be embraced because it requires you to think through exactly what you're building, who is responsible for what parts, and to make sure all parties are clear on the project goal, product deliverables, and timeline.

Jon Nastor on contracts

"In my case, I have always used lawyer drafted contracts. My theory behind this is that all parties do the hard work of agreeing to terms upfront, which makes them more likely to follow through. Once terms are agreed upon and contracts are signed, all parties now know that there are no thoughts or worries of terms and money, so we can put the contracts away and never have to think about them again.

Also, I feel that having contracts upfront makes the other party realize that you are serious and that your vision for this collaboration is big enough to deem a contract. Why am I wasting the person's time collaborating on a project that I don't think is worth the little bit of upfront cost and work?

I feel that if the person I am attempting to partner with takes too long or delays even getting the terms and contract drafted and signed, then this is a significant indicator that they will also be tough to work with during the project.

In the VP contract, we stated that we can hire another developer if required, due to lack of effort on Mark's part, and those costs will be divided equally amongst us."—Jon Nastor, co-founder of Velocitypage.com

Questions to discuss with collaborators:

Focus	Questions	Answer
Define agree-ments and contracts	What type of arrangement will help us do our best work?	
	What are the pros and cons to writing up a contract	
	How should we handle finances?	
	What happens if someone needs to leave the collabora-tion? How do we handle the project and finances?	

Step 8. Develop conflict resolution strategies

In any collaboration, there is the potential for conflict. Instead of trying to avoid it, you are better served having a process for managing it if or when it happens. Here are key questions to ask if you or your collaborators ever clash:

1. What is the issue or problem here?
2. Where do we agree and not agree? This includes the current conflict, but also outside of it. Are there areas where we do agree?
3. How might we take advantage of the areas where we agree to bring us closer to a solution in the areas where we disagree?
4. What actions do we need to take to move this disagreement forward?

Focusing on identifying the conflict and changing the question from who is right or wrong, to the productive "how do we resolve this conflict and move the project forward," changes the dynamic of the group. The original line of questioning leads to anger, resentment, and the potential for a broken relationship. The latter line of questioning turns conflict into a productive challenge for the project. Using this line of questioning will turn every conflict into a chance for growth and project improvement.

Guy Vincent on how to mitigate conflicts

"It comes down to responsibility. Even if you're taking the lead on the project, people will have differences of opinion. As the leader of a collaboration, it's important to be clear on what you want to do. It's better to make a decision on something that you feel needs to be done for the company rather than being stuck in some kind of perpetual limbo and not making a decision. I witnessed one startup separate the other day because of this. They couldn't make progress because they couldn't decide on a particular course of action.

When two people, collaborators or co-founders, can't agree on the direction for a company, it's going to fail. That decision needs to be made very clearly by someone. I accept that this task comes down to myself as the founder of my company, and if you're the lead on a collaboration, that's your responsibility as well. Of course, you take advice from those around you, and you do your best to create a clear strategy, but it's not that easy. You're constantly pulled in many different directions. It's easy to get stuck inside your head, but you have to bring it back to the fundamentals:

- ✓ 'What are our strengths?'
- ✓ 'Where are we right now?'
- ✓ 'What can we do right now that will have the most impact toward what we want to achieve?'"—Guy Vincent, founder of Publishizer.com

There is always the potential for conflict inside a collaboration, so the key is to avoid it if you can by being very clear on what you're building and why, and if conflict does occur, to find common ground and reorient to your original goal.

Questions to discuss with collaborators:

Focus	Questions	Answer
Conflict resolution strategies	How do we mitigate conflict before we begin work?	
	What types of conflict have each of us experienced? What did you learn from this?	
	If conflict arises, how do we want to handle it as a team?	

Azimuth Check

Once you've connected with a collaborator, it's important to establish, together, the project purpose. You want to establish your agreed upon goal at the outset. Doing so will keep you honest with deadlines, tasks, and objectives. You should discuss roles and responsibilities in all areas of your business, and agree on project parameters before you start creating. Don't be afraid of an official contract; whether you have something in writing, you owe it to your project to define the timeline, goal, and scope of work for all persons involved. Finally, before you get started working together, discuss how you plan to address future conflict. Assume there is a 99% chance of small or large conflict, so having this conversation is crucial before you begin working together.

Take a short break here to take notes and collect your thoughts below before moving onto the next Milestone:

Milestone purpose

Turn your idea into a working business model, define your Minimum Viable Product, and set your collaboration up for success by creating your marketing and product wireframes.

Milestone checklist

- [ ] Build your one page business model
- [ ] Define your Minimum Viable Product
- [ ] Create your marketing and product wireframe

MILESTONE 9

PLAN YOUR PROJECT

By this point, you've developed your idea and connected with one or more collaborators. Now it's time for you and your collaborators to develop a working business model, to define your Minimum Viable Product, and to plan your project through a process called "wireframing."

Let's get to it...

Create your one page business model

At this point, all you and your collaborators have is an *idea* of what you're building. If you've followed the steps up until this point, your idea has been summarized on paper, and you've created some form of working agreement. Before sprinting into production mode, you need to do more analysis to determine the feasibility of the business as a whole (and to refine or modify as need be). For this, we'll use a one page business model framework.

For every collaborative project, I recommend filling out a Lean Canvas. The Lean Canvas is a one page business model developed by Ash Maurya, entrepreneur and bestselling author of *Running Lean.*

The Lean Canvas helps identify all the essential elements of a profitable, lean business. While developed for technology-oriented startups, I've found the Lean Canvas works just as effectively when applied to individual products and services in any industry because it helps to focus your effort on what is most important: identifying exactly what you're building, for whom, and how you'll reach them.

Before we begin, it's important to note that creating your first business model should take no more than 20 minutes. If it takes longer than 20 minutes to create, this is an indicator that you and your collaborators need more time to develop your idea into a proper business model. The good news is that you'll be able to find this clarity by using the Lean Canvas because it is a living document, which you will come back to and adjust as you develop, market, and sell your product.

You can create your first Lean Canvas alone or with your collaborators. If you draft out the first version of your business model alone, share it with your collaborators to get their feedback and input. Once everyone has had a chance to help define each section, conduct a 60 minute strategy call to go over each area to make sure everyone understands the business model.

Whether you choose to use a Lean Canvas or another type of framework, you'll want to clarify the following 10 areas:

1. Ideal Customer
2. Early Adopters
3. Problem

4. Solution
5. Competitors
6. Channels
7. Pricing Options
8. Expenses and Overhead
9. Goal + Metrics
10. Unique Selling Proposition

In the following section, I'll walk you through each of these areas.

Please note: for this section, I'm going to share a single collaborative product I helped develop, market, and sell, instead of sharing multiple case studies of clients, peers, or students. My hope is that a single personal example will make this section easier to follow and implement, as you'll see my process from start to finish.

Ready? Let's get to it.

Step 1. Define your ideal customer

Who are you planning to serve? What does this person look like, talk like, act like?

Your ideal customer (also sometimes referred to as an "avatar," "ideal customer profile," "target audience," or "customer segment") is the person who has the problem your product or service intends to solve, at a price point that is within their ability to pay. The key to developing your ideal customer profile is to be very specific about whom you're targeting.

Here are just a few areas you should cover as you define your ideal customer:

1. Age
2. Gender
3. Nationality
4. Location
5. Interests / Hobbies
6. Education

Use the following space to define your ideal customer:

Why you need to start with your ideal customer profile

Omar Zenhom is the CEO and founder of The $100 MBA, a training platform for aspiring entrepreneurs. In his training material, Zenhom stresses the importance of developing your ideal customer profile and testing your ideas with them as quickly as possible:

"Idea validation starts with the audience. You have to find out who you're serving before you can know you're building the right product. At the end of the day, regardless if you're selling a product or service, you're in the service business. You're serving others. You're helping somebody solve a problem, alleviate a pain, or improve their life.

You look at any successful business, this fact is really at the crux of their success; they are solving or improving somebody's life. You have to understand this concept before you start validating ideas.

So, the first step is to think about: 'who is this product, this service, this business for?'

Understanding this ideal customer is critical. You must understand this audience intimately because they're the ones who are going to validate your idea; they're the ones who are going to tell you, 'Yeah, I'm going to buy that,' or 'No I won't buy that.' or 'I would buy that for this price,' or 'I would buy that if it included this.'

So you need to understand your audience very well. "

Case Study: Defining the High Speed Elite ideal customer

High Speed Elite is a business mastermind, training platform, and community for veteran business owners. I co-founded High Speed Elite with John Lee Dumas (founder of Entrepreneuronfire.com), and Antonio Centeno (founder of Realmenrealstyle.com). When we originally brainstormed our ideal customer, we focused on veterans who were preparing to transition out of the military.

Here's what we came up with:

1. Transitioning Veterans
2. Active duty veterans looking to retire or leave the military
3. Civilian veterans who've made the transition but aren't happy with their current situation and want to improve their life by getting a better job or starting their own business

The problem with this definition is that it's too broad and it doesn't stand out among the crowd. Not every transitioning veteran will care about High Speed Elite, especially if we pander to all veterans. This was the first thing we put down on paper to discuss as a team, and we quickly realized the shortcomings of our business model.

After drafting out the rest of the canvas, we came back to this area and refined our target audience. This is what we came up with:

1. Transitioning vets who have gone through "Boots to Business" TAP (Transition Assistance Program) and want to continue their business education
2. Veterans who have engaged with John, Antonio, or Tom online (which indicates they are interested in online business / entrepreneurship)
3. Veterans who have gone through other online business training programs or courses but haven't gotten the support they need as veterans

As you can see, this definition is much more valuable because it's more specific and actionable. Not only is it much easier to find this group of people because we've specifically identified their interests and where they may hang out (online or off), but we have a better indication of what type of marketing language we should use to attract said customers.

Like all parts of the business model, it's possible to improve your definitions as you go. This was our "good enough" solution to move forward with our project.

Step 2. Define early adopters

Who will be your first 100 customers? Who will be your first 1,000 customers?

Too often, I see aspiring entrepreneurs, artists, and writers completely ignore their first (and most important) customers. Most of us believe we know intuitively who our product or service is for, but unless you can specifically define the first 100 or first 1,000 customers, you may find yourself in a situation where you've built something but nobody is buying.

If you're launching a project from scratch, with no audience and few resources, you'll need to be specific with who your early adopters are. And you want to be as detailed as possible about how you'll *reach* your first 100 and first 1,000 customers (which we'll cover in more depth in Step 6: Marketing Channels).

Use the following space to define your early adopters:

Case Study: Defining the High Speed Elite early adopters

Early adopters are the most important part of a new product launch. These are the people who believe in you enough to part with their money, in some cases before the product is even built (we'll talk more about that part later). You should not take these people for granted.

For High Speed Elite, we were fortunate enough to know exactly where we would get our first 100 customers:

1. Antonio's network (blog / youtube)
2. John's network (blog / podcast)
3. Tom's network (blog)

All three of us are veterans who run our own successful businesses. All three of us have existing platforms and are considered thought leaders in our respective spaces. This gave us an unfair advantage when it came to reaching veterans because many veterans had already found us through the work we were each doing on our individual platforms.

To specifically identify our early adopters, we set up a free webinar for veterans and shared it with our platforms. This resulted in over 100 signups for our first launch (enough to launch our product and reach our funding goal).

Even if you don't have an existing platform, specifically think through how you'll reach your earliest customers and future biggest fans.

Step 3. Define the problem

What problem does your ideal customer have? Is the problem obvious? Do they know they have this problem? What is their current solution?

In order to sell anything, you need to have a clear idea what it is your product or service is doing for the customer. This means defining the particular problem your product or service is solving. Specifically, you want to define the problem, determine if the customer knows he or she has the problem, and identify whether they can afford it.

There are two amatuer mistakes made at this point:

1. Assuming the problem exists
2. Identifying a problem that exists, but not one your ideal customer really wants to or cares to fix (at least not at a price point that makes it economically viable for you)

When developing your business model, the best proof that you're identifying a real pain point is to talk to your ideal customers (30-50 conversations should give you statistical validation) and find out if they have a solution they are currently paying for. In the next several Milestones, we will validate and refine this problem. For right now, get as detailed as possible based on the product / market research you've already conducted in Milestone 5: Develop Your Profitable Idea.

Use the following space to define your customer's problem:

Case Study: Defining the High Speed Elite ideal customer problem

For High Speed Elite, we knew the problem of our ideal customer intimately: it's the veteran who has left the military or is planning to leave, and wants to start (or grow) a business.

Our original problem definition looked like this:

1. Veterans are leaving the military unequipped for the civilian world
2. Current Transition Assistance Programs don't cut it—veterans deserve better transition support / help, especially those looking to start or grow a business.
3. The military is cutting their forces dramatically and vets are being flushed into the civilian world—many end up unemployed or underemployed; entrepreneurship could provide a

solution for this that is good for them, our country, and our economy

As we developed our business model and moved forward with our launch, we were able to have more conversations with veterans interested in starting a business. Because of this, we were able to further define our ideal customer's problem:

1. Current government programs to help veterans start businesses don't go beyond the basics; veterans who have little business experience need more hands-on help to start and grow a 6-figure or more business
2. Current business programs for veterans focus on small mom-and-pop style local businesses, not online businesses leveraging new media and technology; veterans who want to start online businesses, lifestyle design businesses, or simply grow and expand through digital marketing are out of luck with current solutions
3. Currently, there are no entrepreneurship programs run by veterans who are operating million dollar businesses; we can walk the walk and talk the talk, which is important to veterans

This gave us enough information to move forward with our project.

Step 4. Outline the solution

How does your product or service solve your ideal customer's problem? How is it different than what is already available? Is the difference valuable (as in, does the difference create better results than current solutions)?

At this point, you want to have an understanding of how you can solve your ideal customer's problem, as well as a general idea of what it will take to create this solution. Draft out how you propose to solve the problem in as much detail as possible. Focus on the key features of your product, removing anything that isn't absolutely necessary.

Use the following space to define your solution:

Case Study: Defining the High Speed Elite solution

This is how we defined our proposed solution for High Speed Elite:

1. In-depth, multi-level training course combined with live office-hour calls + exclusive / private community
2. Access to proven veteran entrepreneurs who've started from scratch and built six and seven figure businesses
3. DIY course (learn and grow at your own pace)
4. Additional mentorship available

We essentially kept this solution the same when it came time to open the doors to High Speed Elite, and based on pre-orders, we had developed the right solution for the right problem.

Step 5. Identify competitors

What are current solutions available to your ideal customer right now?

"Where there is no competition, there is no market."—Geoffrey A. Moore, *Crossing the Chasm*

We've alluded to this in both the problem and solution areas above, but now we need to get very clear on exactly who the competitors are in the space you want to enter. The purpose of identifying competitors isn't to figure out how to beat them at their own game (not yet at least), but to figure out:

1. Is there a market? If there are multiple competitors in the space, you can be sure there's value in what you're creating because people are already paying for solutions.
2. How do they reach their ideal customers? This will give you valuable information on how you might want to approach your ideal customers (or even better, how you can differentiate yourself in the marketplace and focus on a different segment of customers).

Use the following space to identify your competitors:

Case Study: Defining High Speed Elite competitors

For High Speed Elite, there wasn't much competition online in the veteran-specific niche. While we found many veteran-focused business podcasts, blogs, and more, we only found a few courses, programs, or business masterminds. Because of the pedigree of our founders, we figured we'd be able to corner the market with a "blue ocean" strategy; i.e. entering an uncontested market, but one with enough demand to make it profitable.[1]

Step 6. Define your channels

How will you reach your ideal customer and early adopters?

The ability to reach your customer cost-effectively will make or break your business. "Channels" refer to means by which you reach your customers; marketing channels, sales channels, and distribution channels. To clarify, marketing channels are the avenues, platforms, and mediums you use to market, promote, or advertise your products or services to your ideal customer; sales channels are the avenues, platforms, and mediums you use to sell your product to your ideal customers; distribution channels are the avenues, platforms, and mediums you use to deliver your good or service to your ideal customer.

In some cases, a single channel can encompass all three. For example, Amazon.com can be a marketing, sales, and distribution channel because it has a built in customer base of millions. However, even though Amazon can encompass all three channels, it may not be the most effective marketing channel. So if you're selling on Amazon, it would be worthwhile to find alternative marketing channels to reach your ideal customers.

Use the following space to define the channels for your product:

Case Study: Defining the High Speed Elite marketing channels

For High Speed Elite, we decided that, beyond reaching out to our current network and email list to recruit potential students, we'd make Facebook advertising our primary marketing channel. From there, we would host a live webinar and sell our program (sales channel).

Through Facebook ads, we were able to reach a very specific audience. Initially, we started with military in general, eventually niching down to the particular service branches, certain age groups, and certain ranks or degrees. After our first launch, we noticed the majority of our students were either officers or E-6 or above NCOs. This helped us refine our marketing for our second launch, and niche down even further (we used Facebook ads for our second launch as well).

Step 7. Define your pricing options

How do you plan to price and sell your product or service?

It's valuable to look at what the market is already paying for current solutions. This should give you an idea of what people are already willing and able to pay. There are two ways to differentiate yourself in the marketplace in terms of pricing: move up or down. My recommendation: use your competitor's pricing as your base price and figure out how you can provide more value while charging a higher price. If you choose to go the discount route, you enter the race to the bottom:

"The problem with the race to the bottom is that you might win."—Seth Godin

Use the following space to outline your pricing options:

Case Study: Defining the High Speed Elite pricing model

To decide our pricing model, we looked at two things: value creation (what value our product or service would create) and market positioning. We ended up deciding on a $3,000 price tag for 6 months of weekly mentorship, one-on-one calls, an MBA level course, with lifetime access to everything we build inside High Speed Elite.

Here's our reasoning:

First, we knew there was only one way to make High Speed Elite successful, and that was to price high. There are already dozens, maybe hundreds of programs out there for military servicemen and women that are free or cheap. We didn't want to play in that arena. We knew we had to differentiate right from the start, and specifically in relation to pricing.

Second, as veterans, we recognized the need for one-on-one mentorship and guidance from proven veteran entrepreneurs. Many programs directed towards veterans in this space are taught by teachers without real life experience. Conversely, all three of us were running six or seven figure businesses. In other words, we had been in the shoes of our ideal customer, something we discovered was important to them as we started to have conversations with prospective students.

We also knew that there were very few people attempting to charge veterans for services in this realm. Since there's no business if there's no revenue, we decided to start at a premium price. This was also essential because we were using The Lean Launch Technique (we'll cover this in the following section), so we needed enough up front investment from students to properly build the platform without going into debt.

Our pricing resulted in less total students entering our program, but the caliber of student was high (i.e. more engaged, faster learners, etc.). Further, less students meant less overall time investment, which made the choice to go premium a good one for us.

Step 8. Define expenses and overhead

What will it take to fully deliver on the promise you're making with your product or service?

When estimating expenses and overhead, make sure to include not only cost of resources—sunk costs and recurring expenses—but time and labor necessary to finish and ship your product. While you don't need to have exact figures at this time, you should do your due diligence to figure out how much time and money you're going to need to invest to bring this product to life.

At this point, you should have an idea of expected time and money it will take to build and sell your product. You don't need to get too detailed here, but use this as a reference point as you develop your plan.

Use the following space to define expenses and overhead:

Case Study: Defining High Speed Elite expenses and overhead

Defining expenses at the outset of a project can be incredibly difficult. First, because you don't have historical records to calculate anticipated expenses. Second, because depending on what you're offering, it's tough to gauge overhead and recurring expenses to continue operation.

For High Speed Elite, our breakdown looked like this:

> People Cost: $1,000 / person / month = $3,000 (?)
>
> Business Expenses (affiliate, ecommerce solution, membership site, upkeep) = $1,000 per month (?)
>
> Break Even = $4,000 / month; $24,000 / 6 months
>
> Business Mastermind Course @ $3,000 = 1.5 sales / month; 8 sales / 6 months

Our expenses ended up being distributed differently, but the overall expenses to build, maintain, and operate our program ended up costing about $10,000-$15,000 for the first six months, and about $5,000 for the next six because the infrastructure was built. In the end, our rough estimates ended up being about right, which was enough for us to move forward with the launch.

Step 9. Define your goals and metrics

What does success look like to you? What specifically are you trying to do? Most importantly, is there a way to properly measure this result?

When defining your goals and metrics, I recommend defining one goal and one metric to measure and determine the success (or failure) of your goal. If you can't clearly define your goal and measure your results, there's no way to tell if you're moving in the right direction.

For this section, get as specific as you can with your goal, and make sure the metric you use to measure success or failure is directly correlated with the achievement of your goal. For example, if your goal is a net revenue amount, your success metric could be sales. If your goal is growth, your success metric could be subscribers. Each one of these metrics works because they correlate to the goal.

Use the following space to define your goals and metrics:

Case Study: Defining High Speed Elite goals

Our goal with High Speed Elite was to help 10 veterans build cash flowing businesses over the course of 12-24 months. Our goal was to reach 10 students and $30,000 for our first launch. We also established a minimum number we needed to make the "stop / go" decision with our program; if we could not reach our minimum funding goal (4 students and $12,000 in revenue), we would consider canceling the program and refunding whatever money we raised. Luckily, while we didn't reach our funding goal, we didn't have to cancel the program (we were just shy of our goal). Better yet, our next launch allowed us to reach our goal (and with less time and energy investment because we had built all our systems during the first launch).

Step 10. Define your unique selling proposition

What differentiates your product in the marketplace, and what makes your product stand out to your ideal customer in a way that matters?

"In a way that matters" may be the key criterion for this particular area.

Does it matter to your ideal customer if the educational course you're creating was inspired by your time at home school? Or is it more important that the interface is intuitive, students can easily manage and track their progress, and the instruction itself is top notch?

Does it matter to your ideal customer if the magazine you're publishing was edited by some big name editor? Or is it more important that you publish engaging content, high-quality images, and highlight the best and brightest in your industry?

Does it matter to your ideal customer if the software you're creating runs on Django? Or is it more important that it does whatever it promises to do, better and more cost effectively than the alternative?

The point isn't that these particular differences I'm using as examples are irrelevant. Who knows—maybe they ARE important to your ideal customer. The point I'm making is that you need to get clarity on what makes you different in a way that matters to your ideal customer.

Use the following space to define your unique selling proposition:

Case Study: Defining the High Speed Elite unique selling proposition (USP)

Here's how we defined High Speed Elite's USP at the start:

> *An in-depth, full-featured veterans transition success course + exclusive community to help veterans get their dream job or build their own from scratch, built by veterans who've been where you've been.*

As you can see, we started with a focus on all veterans, but eventually shifted gears, focusing entirely on aspiring entrepreneurs and business owners. We eventually refined this to the following:

> *A premium business mastermind for veterans who want to start or grow a six to seven figure businesses, led by proven veteran entrepreneurs.*

The difference that mattered to our ideal customer was being involved in a veteran-led mastermind by people who had built six and seven figure businesses.

Business model summary

As you can see, creating your first business model is a bit of a guessing game. You may not know all the answers, but putting your ideas to paper will help you get definiteness of purpose, and allow you and your collaborators to explore the key aspects of your business. Make sure you sit down and iterate your business model at least once with all your teammates so everyone agrees on the premise of what you're working on, why, and how. From here onward, you should continue to reference your business model and update it as you begin to validate your business model.

Define your Minimum Viable Product

Now that you have a working business model, it's time to define exactly what it is you will be building. This takes us to building a Minimum Viable Product (MVP). The term Minimum Viable Product was coined by Frank Robinson, made popular by Steve Blank, and later made mainstream by Eric Ries, author of *The Lean Startup.*

There have been many definitions of what makes a Minimum Viable Product. For the purposes of online product launches and collaboration, we'll define the Minimum Viable Product as: "the simplest version of a product or service that solves the problem of your ideal customer completely."

The question then becomes: *how do we know what the "simplest" version of a product or service looks like?*

The answer is through validation...

Validating your MVP

"It's critical to understand that an MVP is not the product with fewer features. Rather it is the simplest thing that you can show to customers to get the most learning at that point in time. Early on in a startup, an MVP could simply be a PowerPoint slide, wireframe, clay model, sample data set, etc. Each time you build an MVP you also define what you are trying to test/measure. Later, as more is learned, the MVP's go from low-fidelity to higher fidelity, but the goal continues to be to maximize learning not to build a beta/fully featured prototype of the product."—Steve Blank[2]

Before diving into exactly how to build your Minimum Viable Product, it's important to note that the fundamental purpose of the MVP is *learning.*

In other words, how do you quickly and cheaply find out what it is your ideal customer wants and will pay for?

And the fastest, cheapest way to find out what your ideal customer wants and will pay for is to "progressively validate" your MVP.

"Progressively validating" your MVP means testing your idea in incremental stages instead of waiting until you have your ultimate, final product, ready to sell.

If you apply this principle to your collaboration, you will naturally begin to seek out ways to test your ideas throughout the product development process. Taken to its edge, this means pre-selling your product before it's built. I'll show you exactly how to do that in this section and in the coming Milestones and Phases. For now, let's start with the philosophy behind pre-selling as progressive validation of your business idea.

Pre-selling and The Lean Launch Technique

The traditional factory-model approach to building a new product is as follows:

1. Idea
2. Build
3. Test
4. Sell

5. Deliver
6. Learn (keep selling or build something new)

While this was an effective way for big companies to develop and launch new products in the industrial economy of the 20th century, it's not conducive to bootstrappers and collaborators who have limited time, money, and resources. After all, what if your idea doesn't sell after hundreds or thousands spent on development? The reality isn't pretty.

The good news is, with the advent of cheap technology and unparalleled worldwide connection, it is possible to flip this model on its head.

The Lean Launch Technique I propose is as follows:

1. Idea
2. Sell
3. Learn
4. Build
5. Deliver

In other words, we put an emphasis on learning by moving as quickly to the selling phase as possible, saving the building of said product for later (and removing the "test" phase altogether because we do that in real-time with our customers). This reduces waste by letting us know as soon as possible whether an idea is worth building in the first place.

Like Ash Maurya says: "life's too short to build something nobody wants."[3]

Which means if you want to spend time building important things that matter to people, you need to validate your idea as quickly as possible.

The fastest way to do this is by pre-selling.

A caveat: pre-selling may not work for every product or service. Some products must be full-featured with all the kinks worked out from the start, like defibrillators and passenger planes (in order to pre-sell either of those, you would need a lot of klout in your industry). On the other hand, almost every product or service you or I will be building in a business-to-consumer context that isn't life or death can be validated most effectively by pre-selling. Thus, less waste of time, money, and resources, and more time to over-deliver on your original promise.

Case Study: progressively validating an idea through crowdfunding

You don't have to look much further than the popularization of crowdfunding to see just how powerful it can be to sell an idea before you build it. Not to mention, how acceptable this is to the majority of people. This book is a great case study. I crowdfunded this book when I had the idea for it. Instead of spending a year writing it, and then another 6 months launching it, hoping I'd make back my investment (fat chance), I decided to outline the book, create a sales page on Publishizer.com, and then let my audience know they could preorder the book.

There was also a caveat—if I didn't raise $7,500 I wouldn't write the book. That was the minimum amount of money I needed to pay for editors, formatters, designers, and distribution. It was also the metric I used to determine interest. If enough people were interested in the idea, $7,500 would not be a hard number to reach. Conversely, if I couldn't reach $7,500, that would tell me the book shouldn't be written. I ended up raising $12,979 before writing a word of the book.[4]

Idea = validated. And better yet, my risk is reduced to almost zero, assuming I can deliver on the original promise.

But what if people pay?

The interesting thing about The Lean Launch Technique is this: instead of the issue being "what if nobody buys?" the concern becomes "what if people do buy?"

That's a good worry to have, isn't it?

The solution is simple, albeit unconventional (and may feel uncomfortable if this is your first time trying it). Here's what you do:

1. Share your MVP—just the shell of what you're creating with your ideal customer (we'll discuss how to do this in the next Phase)
2. Pitch the product with a discount for early adopters, letting them know the discount is because the product is in development
3. Accept payment

A lot of people are nervous about selling. The idea of selling something that isn't created yet can be even more intimidating. However, by selling on a promise, you force yourself to rise to the occasion and produce your best (and fastest) work.

How many projects have you procrastinated on because you weren't held accountable? Inevitably, the deadline comes around and you pull something out of thin air. While the experience is rarely pleasant (all-nighters are brutal for everyone), you got it done. How? More importantly, is there any way to replicate this demand without waiting until the last minute?

When you accept payment on a promise, you won't let the people you serve down. This is an incredibly powerful motivator and a great way to keep yourself accountable.

As a side note: do not spend the money you receive from early adopters. Make sure you always have enough in savings to refund if the project goes south. You'll find most early adopters are forgiving of failure, although this certainly isn't something you want to take advantage of.

Questions to help you define your Minimum Viable Product

Focus	Questions	Answer
Minimum Viable Product	What is the end product I'm building, and how does it solve the customer's problem?	
	How do I know this product will solve the customer's problem?	
	What are the critical features of the product—the ones necessary to solve the customer's problem? Which features are nice, but not critical?	
	What else can I remove from this product while still solving the customer's problem?	

Wireframe your project

Now that you've been able to brainstorm your Minimum Viable Product, it's time to turn your ideas into an actionable framework. This requires building a "wireframe"—a visual representation of what you're delivering and how.

There are two types of wireframes you'll need to create:

#1. The marketing and sales wireframe

The marketing and sales wireframe shows how your customers will find you and how you will deliver your product or service; think of it as a robust user flow model, that shows how the customer finds out about you, how they get to your website, what they have to click through to find and buy your product, and then how that product will be delivered to them.

#2. The product wireframe

The product wireframe is the shell of your product. This could start as a few sketches on a piece of paper that you turn into a working sales page, which shows all the components of your product and corresponding benefits to the customer for using them.

A successful product wireframe not only outlines all the components of a product, but does so in a way that it could be presented to a potential customer and get him or her interested in buying. This is exactly what we'll do in Milestone 12

Why you need a wireframe

The objective of both the sales and marketing wireframe and the product wireframe is to give a visual snapshot of what you're building and how it works in order to reduce uncertainty and ambiguity among collaborators, which could otherwise slow down your product development and launch.

While a thorough outline is necessary for building a Task List (covered in the next Milestone), using only a written outline can lead to missing steps and requirements, especially in the context of collaboration where you're working with multiple people. It's important to remember you're working with team members, and how you understand an outline is going to be different than how your collaborators understand the same outline. Too often, solopreneurs (and doomed-to-fail collaborations) begin building before they have a full grasp of the resources necessary to deliver on their vision. Creating a wireframe of your product and marketing and sales process will help you identify precisely what you'll need to build so you can identify and source the right tools and software to create it.

How to create your sales and marketing wireframe

For the marketing and sales wireframe, you'll want to outline the progressive stages of the launch, as well as the type of advertising and marketing you want to use.

Use the following questions to brainstorm and outline your sales and marketing wireframe:

What is the path of the user? How and where will she learn about your product? What action must she take to learn more or sign up? How does she actually buy the product?

What web pages do you need to create? What is the key call-to-action on each one and where does it lead? What happens if someone leaves one of the pages before completing the call-to-action?

What software is necessary to make each step happen? Do you need hosting? WordPress installed? An eCommerce solution to accept credit cards?

What are the main selling points that need to be made along the way? Are there any particular marketing collaterals you or your team need to create (i.e. Facebook advertising images? Images of your product or service? Marketing copy for your sales page?)

How to create your product wireframe

For the product wireframe (i.e. the digital product you'll be delivering), you'll need to outline the essential features of the product, what it looks like, how it works, how it should be operated, and how the customer will get it into his or her hands.

Questions to consider as you develop your product wireframe:

What does the final product look like from the outside? What does the packaging (digital or physical) look like?

What does the final product look like from the inside? When the ideal customer is using it (e.g. it's User Interface or UI)?

How does it work? What is the best way for the customer to operate this particular product? What must he or she do to get it up and running?

What are the essential features of the software? What are the essential elements of the product when it's in the customer's hands (i.e. do you really need all those buttons? Do you need all those options to be present? Can you deliver the product in incremental stages? Would that improve it?

Use the following pages to wireframe your marketing and sales process:

Marketing and sales wireframe continued:

Marketing and sales wireframe continued:

Marketing and sales wireframe continued:

Marketing and sales wireframe continued:

Marketing and sales wireframe continued:

Tools for wireframing

Sketching out your wireframe by hand is a great place to start, but not great for collaborative work. The following pieces of software can help with the wireframing process:

Office 365 / Google Docs

The Microsoft Office suite of tools, including Word and PowerPoint, are all you really need to craft your product wireframe and product delivery wireframe (the examples in this book were built in PowerPoint). The downside is that file sharing and collaborating on the same document at the same time isn't as intuitive as Google Docs.

Like Microsoft's Office 365, Google Docs has everything you need to outline and wireframe your product, including Docs (a Word equivalent), Sheets (an Excel equivalent), Slides (a PowerPoint equivalent), and more. The best part is that it's a completely free, cloud based solution, which makes it ideal for remote work and collaboration. It's also very easy to track changes, edits, and more (another bonus for collaborative work).

Trello

Trello is a simple, powerful, and free project management tool. Trello will help you organize and manage multiple projects, whether solo or collaboratively. Trello is organized into the hierarchy of Boards, Lists, and Cards. Your project Board will include all the content related to our project. As you begin to wireframe your project using Trello, use a combination of Lists and Cards to develop the individual pieces of your project.

Evernote

Evernote is a robust note taking tool. With Evernote, you can capture thoughts on the fly, save and draw over webpages, take pictures and screen captures and annotate them from your phone or computer, and much more. Best of all, it seamlessly syncs between devices and is compatible with just about every major platform and most pieces of hardware available at retailers (so just about anyone can use this tool).

During the process of writing this book, I used Evernote not only as a research tool (to save all my notes, references, and sources in one spot) but also as an outline, wireframe, and rough draft development tool.

Case Study: Wireframing a membership site

In late 2014, I collaboratively launched a new publishing training course, community, and book launch platform called Publishers' Empire. The goal of Publishers' Empire is to help authors create, package, and sell more books. After brainstorming and planning the project, we knew it would include a membership-style interface, over 100 HD videos, a 24/7 community, resources, templates, and live training.

We then took this concept and wireframed what the product sales and marketing process would look like, as well as what the actual deliverable would look like (product wireframe).

Here's what we came up with:

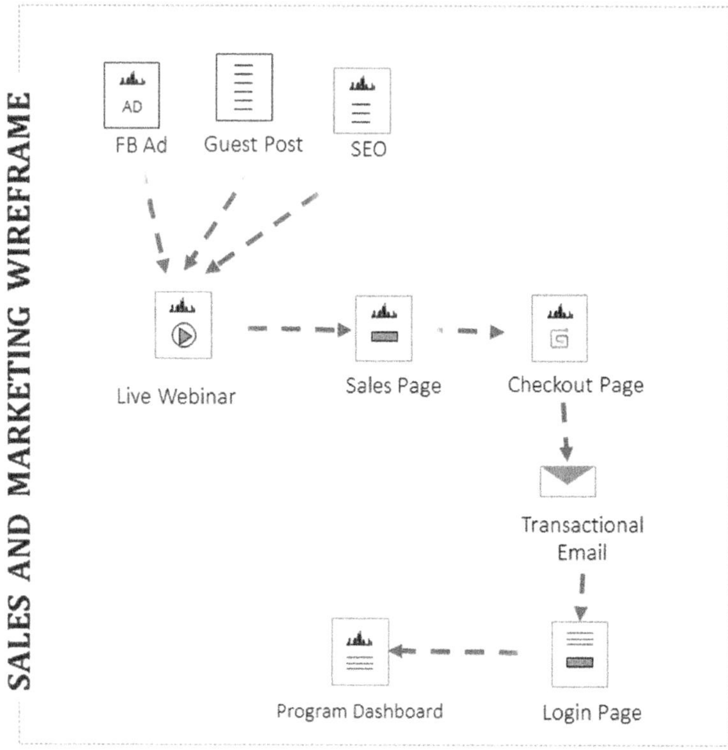
SALES AND MARKETING WIREFRAME
AD
FB Ad
Guest Post
SEO
Live Webinar
Sales Page
Checkout Page
Transactional Email
Login Page
Program Dashboard

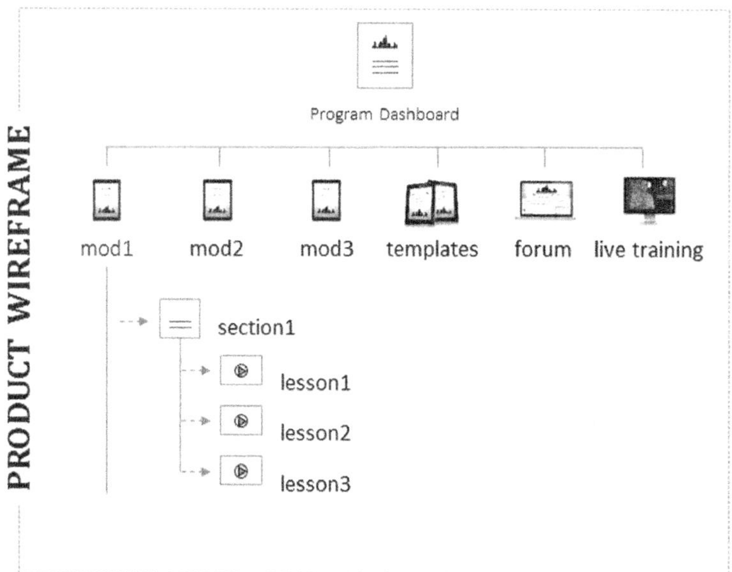
PRODUCT WIREFRAME
Program Dashboard
mod1
mod2
mod3
templates
forum
live training
section1
lesson1
lesson2
lesson3

The above wireframe is essentially a flow model of how a user will find, buy, and then move through my program, which helps me to identify every single page I need to create as well as what technology is necessary to make this happen. I always like to focus on the practical elements, specifically: what type of pages I'll need to build, how they will connect, what emails will need to go out and when, how I'll receive payment from the customer, etc.

Case Study: Validating an MVP by pre-selling

Because I'm in the publishing space, I'm constantly working with authors to help them create, package, and sell books. Naturally, I find certain areas of publishing are more crucial to success than others. Promotion is one of these areas. If an author does not know how to promote himself, how can he sell books? By paying attention to the needs of my ideal customer, I am able to identify promotion as a bottleneck to author success.

The question I need to answer is: how can I rapidly create and test this idea before spending hundreds of hours and thousands of dollars building the first prototype? Here's how I did it:

Step 1. Develop the idea

One of the ways I help authors break through a promotional bottleneck is through strategic outreach to connect them with media publishers (bloggers, podcasters, etc.). I do this for authors I publish, but because I only publish a few books a year, I have the capacity to do this activity for more authors. It seemed like a good idea to do a spinoff business where I help authors with marketing and promoting their books, with the goal of putting their book sales on autopilot.

Step 2. Outline and wireframe

Immediately, I outlined the steps I would take to complete the task for the author. This routine took the form of 5 bullet points I used to address my ideal customer. Here's what it looked like:

> *How Bookblitz Works*
>
> *Step 1. Decide how many influencers (anyone with an audience, such as bloggers, podcasters, radio show hosts, publishers, etc.) you want us to reach out to for you (we call these "engagements")*
>
> *Step 2. Flip the switch (purchase)*
>
> *Step 3. Fill out your Bookblitz Debrief Form, which tells us about you and your book (sent immediately following subscription)*
>
> *Step 4. Bookblitz will develop a unique book marketing strategy for your book, which we'll review with you before we precede (and make any necessary changes or adjustments)*
>
> *Step 5. Bookblitz goes to work, finding and connecting you with media outlets to promote you and your book (think: interviews, book promos, giveaways, speaking engagements—all based on the requirements you set in the Bookblitz Debrief Form)*
>
> *Step 6. Sit back in your hammock and enjoy an ice cold margarita while influencers and publishers from around the world knock at your door to promote and share your book with their audiences.*

I also wireframed the marketing and sales process, as well as the product itself. Because I was intending to use my pre-existing social media audience, I knew I would find my users on a particular Facebook group. I would then direct message interested parties. From there, I would send them a very simple sales page I could build in LeadPages.net, and sell them my service through Gumroad.com.

Step 3. Build the team

I already had a small team through Insurgent Publishing, so I didn't have to do anything here. However, if I were starting from scratch, I would look for people who could help facilitate the outreach process (individuals good at cold calling, cold emailing, closing sales, etc.). At this point, I would merely propose what I believe to be possible from a marketing and sales standpoint, as well as what I predict the financial upside to be. Before moving forward, I would develop a basic contract that included the Scope of Work for all parties. This would ensure everyone was on the same wavelength before moving forward.

Step 4. Test the idea

Next, I shared the idea on a Facebook group, posing it as a question with a hypothetical solution. Here's the exact post:

> *"Need feedback...*
>
> *If you're an author, would you be interested in being connected with podcasters, bloggers (and possibly radio shows, television, mainstream media) in relevant niches in order to market and promote your book?*
>
> *From a practical standpoint, this service would define relevant marketing segments based on your book, then develop 'outreach lists' where we find potential podcasts and bloggers in your niche, and then actually facilitate the outreach for you.*
>
> *Basically, you pay for the service, and out comes introductions to bloggers and podcasters, to either (1) be on their pod-*

cast, (2) do a guest post, (3) get a book review they'll share with their audiences.

Would this be a service you would use?

I've been playing around with this idea for a while because I keep seeing people pay for marketing gigs like Fiverr to have someone blanket blast their book on generic FB pages. I know this can work to some degree, but it does nothing to build consistent, ongoing sales.

The only way to generate consistent, ongoing sales of books is to focus on LONGTAIL marketing (i.e. blogs, podcasts, etc. that can continue to funnel new people your way...plus, it's great for SEO).

Further, based on some of my recent campaigns, I've received response rates upwards of 55%, with positive responses (yes, we'd like you on the podcast or yes, we'd like to review your book, or yes we'd like you to guest post) as high as 38%.

This means that of the 100 channels we approached, 38 will promote the book in some way, shape, or form. That's 38 separate websites and blogs promoting a single book, over the course of several weeks / months.

Anyway, just a proposition.

This is the first stage of validation for this idea to see if it has legs.

If you're interested, let me know.

If you hate the idea, but you pay for fiverr services, please let me know what you hate about this idea and why fiverr is better.

And if you like to party, keep doing that too."

This simple, grammatically incorrect post resulted in over 60 comments. Some of them like this:

> *"'Tom, late to the thread but I'm in. I actually just paid a bunch to a VA to get blogger and traditional media hits from my 'competitors' for my next book...and they didn't even do a very good job. Getting ready to drop coin on a Podcast booking service... but drop me an email or setup a call if you think you could have this in place very soon.'*
>
> *'Love this idea Tom. This seems to be something that will fill a hole in the author market. So basically, you would be like a publicist for indie authors that normally wouldn't have access to one, which would also create another reason to do away with being at the mercy of the big time publishers, or to help save authors from having do all of the leg work on their own....I would be happy to be one of your guinea pigs if you still need one and if I would fit your author criteria. Either way, I support your idea.'*
>
> *'Tom, it's sounds good (like too good to be true). This would be perfect for indie authors. I know it's effective, I just don't do it because I can't do all. I second Angela with everything she said and I would love to be a piggy too.'"*

Step 5. Sell

The next thing my team and I did: accept payment for our service. Instead of going back and building the platform, the sales page, or anything else like that, we simply gave people a purchase form through Gumroad.com. We ended up with four customers in the first week.

Summary

The outline of the Bookblitz service, in conjunction with the the Gumroad.com payment form, was our Minimum Viable Product. By posting on Facebook and receiving positive feedback, we began to validate that the need existed. Next, we had to validate whether our ideal customer (indie-authors) would pay. By simply offering the Gumroad.com payment form, we had our first customer within 48 hours, and three customers within five days.

All of this we did with no sales page and no marketing push—just an idea that we progressively validated through a conversation on Facebook, followed by asking people to pay for services to be rendered.

How to create your next MVP validation test

Scaling is a term often used by technology startups to describe the act of growing a company's user base or revenue. In this case, scaling is finding, selling, and providing this service for *many more* authors. For example, helping three authors is great, but could we reach 10 in the next 30 days? If so, the next question would be, can we reach 100 in the next 90 days?

Each one of these questions forces our team to build and test a new MVP. For example, the next MVP would be to build a proper sales page and to start promoting it through other channels. If I can't reach 10 customers in 30 days, I may need to go back to the drawing board and evaluate the business, or Pivot to test something else. Regardless of the results of each MVP test, by establishing a goal and defining our success criteria, we can iteratively build and test MVPs in the marketplace, with each one helping us get closer to our final "whole solution" product (in much less time, money, and effort than producing everything in the beginning, and then waiting weeks, months, or years to sell the completed project).

Azimuth Check

Turning your idea into a one page business model will give you and your collaborators clarity and direction as you go forward. From here, you can define your Minimum Viable Product, or the simplest product that will solve your ideal customer's problem completely. With an MVP in hand, you can now create your product wireframe and sales and marketing wireframes. At this point, you have everything you need to turn your vision into a step-by-step plan and timeline, which we'll create in the next Milestone.

To get acess to bonus resources and digital templates from this Milestone, go to: www.tommorkes.com/collaborate

Take a short break here to take notes or add your thoughts below before moving onto the next Milestone:

Milestone purpose

To turn your wireframe into Objectives and Task Lists, to develop a timeline, and to begin work on your product in an organized, efficient manner.

Milestone checklist

- ☐ Define Objectives, Task Lists, and create your timeline
- ☐ Understand the 80/20 principle and how to apply it to your project
- ☐ Manage your team to stay on track

MILESTONE 10

DEVELOP YOUR PRODUCT

At this point, you have:

1. Assembled your team
2. Established roles, responsibilities, and the scope of work of your project
3. Come to an agreement and understanding of how the project will progress and how you'll deal with conflict should it arise
4. Developed your one page business model
5. Defined your Minimum Viable Product
6. Created your product and sales and marketing wireframes

Now it's time to turn your wireframe into a Objectives and Task Lists, to create your timeline, and to begin building your product and sales funnel (while keeping your team on track).

Let's get to it.

Step 1. Commit to your launch date

When planning a military operation, leaders follow a process called backward planning. Backward planning involves defining exactly what you want to happen by a certain date and time, and then working backward to fill in the blanks of what must be accomplished to reach this desired end-state. This means you need to set and commit to your launch date before beginning.

Write down your launch date (and any other relevant dates) below:

Step 2. Collaboratively review your desired end-state

An "end-state" is a term used in the US Military to describe the situation at the end of a mission (e.g. what is the status of enemy and friendly forces, where are they located, what does the environment look like now, how do we know we've reached this point, etc.). The desired end-state is the best possible final result of your project. The difference between a desired end-state and a goal is that your goal is just one part of your end-state, and by defining and reviewing your desired end-state with your collaborators, you'll have a clear picture of everything that must be accomplished to get to that point.

For High Speed Elite, our desired end-state was a $30,000 launch (either that amount in a bank account or spread out in payments over six months), all students registered into our system, the course material ready for consumption, and our program onboarding sequence initiated.

For your collaboration, the desired end-state could be completely different. To determine the best possible final result of a project, you need to clarify the following:

1. Goal
2. Project deliverables
3. Metrics for success

Most of these items have been identified either from your brainstorming sessions outlined earlier in this book, or in the one page business model you created in Milestone 9. While this section might seem redundant, it's important to revisit essential aspects of your project throughout the entire process (from ideation through the launch).

Use the following sections to discuss each of these areas with your collaborators to make sure everyone is on the same wavelength before moving forward.

1. Goal

What is the goal of this project?

What specific, positive outcome do you want to achieve?

What personal goals do you have in relation to the project?

How do these individual goals impact the overarching goal of the project?

2. Project deliverables

What is the final deliverable? What is the thing that reaches the customer's hand?

How does he or she receive your product or service?

What follow up steps are necessary to ensure the customer receives the full value from your product or service?

3. Metrics for success

How do you measure success or failure?

What is the single variable you intend to measure?

How does it relate to your overarching goal?

Step 3. Outline Key Objectives

A Key Objective is anything that must be done to create, market, sell, and ship your product. For example, with High Speed Elite, several of our Key Objectives included:

1. Creating the sales page
2. Creating the webinar slides
3. Hosting our website and finding a solution to deliver the live webinar
4. Finding and integrating an eCommerce solution

Think in terms of final items that need to be created, designed, and deployed (the specific steps to create, design, or deploy these items will be covered next).

How to outline Key Objectives

Starting with your desired end-state, and in conjunction with the wireframe you created in the previous Project Milestone, work your way backward all the way to where you are presently. Ask yourself the following questions:

What are the major objectives required to ship your project? What must get done in order for your finished product to reach the hands of your customer?

Spend 30-60 minutes with your collaborators to brainstorm all the components of your project, and use the space below to draft up an initial list of Key Objectives:

Tools for collaborating:

Like wireframing, identifying Key Objectives is great to do on paper at first, but it helps to quickly move to collaborative software. I recommend one of the following to outline your Key Objectives:

Google Docs

I've already mentioned upsides to Google Docs as a platform to construct your wireframe. On top of this, it's an ideal tool to collaboratively develop your Key Objectives. Google Docs sets itself apart from Microsoft Word by being cloud-based and collaborative from the start. No more editing, saving, uploading, sending, downloading, opening, editing, saving, uploading, sending, cycle here. Instead, you can invite key users to your document and give them permission to contribute, and you can all work on the same document simultaneously.

Secondly, Google Docs integrates nicely with everything Google, from Gmail to Drive. This is nice if you're using Google software to begin with and will make collaborative work that much easier.

You can find Google Docs at: www.docs.google.com

Trello

Trello is more technically a project organization tool or project management tool than writing software, but the tool is robust enough that you can generate simple outlines and wireframes within it. The benefits to using Trello are:

1. Free software. Like Google Docs, Trello is completely free. While they offer a premium version of the software, the free version comes with everything you need to lead and manage a collaborative project.

2. Outline, organize, and manage. Trello is structured using boards, lists, and cards. Cards are placed within lists, and lists within boards. In each card, you can add notes, checklists, due dates, and more. This makes it very easy to use Trello's card feature for Key Objectives.
3. Get a head start on your project. By creating Key Objectives within Trello, you're already prepping your Project Management Board, which is the next step in the process.

You can find Trello at: www.trello.com

Hackpad

Hackpad is a relative newcomer to the online collaborative document world. Released in 2011, it was acquired by Dropbox in 2014, although has yet to be given an overhaul to integrate better with their service, which means it doesn't have quite the versatility of Google Docs. That said, it's a solid and reliable collaborative writing tool. The benefits to using Hackpad:

1. Free software. No need to pay to start working collaboratively.
2. Create powerful checklists. Surprisingly, of all the features Google Docs includes, it forgets one essential component—checkboxes for easy task management. Hackpad has this feature built in so you always know how far along you are with a project.
3. Intuitive interface. Google Docs leaves a lot to be desired from a design and usability standpoint. Hackpad, on the other hand, looks great and works almost flawlessly. It's a much smoother writing experience overall. That said, it doesn't include as many features as Google Docs or Trello, nor as many integrations, so it comes down to personal preference.

You can find Hackpad at: www.hackpad.com

Step 4. Subdivide Key Objectives into Task Lists

A Task List is a list of tasks in chronological order that must be completed sequentially to complete, finish, and/or ship your Key Objective. Every Key Objective can be (and should be) subdivided into a Task List. The purpose of subdividing Key Objectives into Tasks is to reduce ambiguity among collaborators, and to provide a clear path forward.

How to subdivide Key Objectives into Task Lists

Ideally, each Key Objective should be subdivided until every Task takes less than 1 hour to accomplish. This will make assigning Tasks simple and effective; the last thing you want to do is assign an ambiguous Task to a collaborator that leaves too much room for interpretation, because this will devolve into inaction.

Here is an example of one of my Task Lists for this book. One of my objectives was to create and run three webinars. I made this into its own card, and then broke it down into a Task List (the checklist of items under "To Do"):

You do not need to have every Task defined nor ordered sequentially at the start. The goal here is to have a basic glidepath from which you can collaboratively flesh out as the project progresses.

How Publishizer.com creates and assigns tasks

One of the keys to Guy Vincent's success as the CEO Publishizer.com, specifically in regards to managing and leading a remote team, is to develop a process around how they integrate collaborative ideas:

"Once you know what you want to achieve, you have to develop a plan. Once you develop the plan and know the steps involved, then you need to put them into a Task List (we use Trello and create Cards for these), and assign those tasks to whoever it is that needs to execute them. As the leader, you are accountable for making sure everything gets done. That's pretty much my workflow process around deciding what needs to get done and how to get it done."

Tools and software for Task List creation

Todoist

Todoist is a task manager, but it's also useful from a project management standpoint, because you can create and assign tasks to anyone within your team. This tool may be redundant if you're already using Trello, however Todoist comes with the ability to create multiple levels of subtasks making Task List organization much more intuitive.

You can find Todoist at www.todoist.com

Trello

We've talked about Trello before as project management software. Trello includes a checklist feature that allows you to create an infinite number of Tasks in the form of checklists within Trello cards. If you're looking to keep everything under one roof, Trello will help you do this.

You can find Todoist at www.trello.com

Hackpad

We covered Hackpad as a great collaborative writing solution in the previous section. Because Hackpad includes a checklist feature, it works well as a Task List creation tool. However, unlike Todoist and Trello, this is the extent of the features for Hackpad (no assigning a person to a task; no colored labels; no way to shift things around except by copying and pasting; no way to assign due dates, etc.). This makes Hackpad limited in its function as a Task List creation tool. I would only recommend Hackpad if the product you're creating is very straightforward and doesn't require an entire Project Management Board to build.

You can find Hackpad at www.hackpad.com

Step 5. Create your Project Management Board

A bunch of handwritten (or hand-typed) notes is great for brainstorming but it's terrible for managing anything. Once you have your Key Objectives defined and Task Lists developed, it's time to add these to some form of project management software.

For this process, I recommend using collaborative, cloud-based project management software, as this will speed up the process of going from idea to taking action (which is key for a rapid digital product launch). Here are some examples of collaboration-focused project management software:

Trello

Trello offers everything you want from your project management tool, including the ability to invite others, tag particular collaborators with particular tasks, set due dates, organize tasks with customizable labels, share documents, create and execute checklists, and much more.

For the purposes of this book, I'll be using Trello as the project management tool of choice. This will allow you to see exactly how I would structure and lead a collaborative project. Please note, however, that while I'll show you how to use Trello to accomplish what I'm teaching in this book (to make it practical and immediately actionable), the fundamentals are the same no matter what tool you use.

You can find Trello at: www.trello.com

Asana

Asana is a project management tool that allows for task creation with checklists, the ability to organize tasks into projects that you can share and work on collaboratively, and an intuitive commenting system so your ideas don't get lost. Like Trello, you can add attachments, set due dates, and the platform works on most operating systems, including mobile. Asana's goal is to take projects out of your email inbox to facilitate better collaboration, and it does this remarkably well. Asana is free to use for individuals and small teams and starts at only $21 / month for the premium plan with 5 users, so pricing won't break the bank either.

You can find Asana at: www.asana.com

Basecamp

Basecamp is another popular project management tool. Like Trello and Asana, it includes the ability to create and assign tasks, set due dates, and manage multiple projects with multiple teams. Used by thousands of companies around the world, Basecamp starts at $20 / month and is a reliable, minimalist project management tool.

Find Basecamp at: www.basecamp.com

How to structure your Project Management Board

How you decide to structure your Project Management Board is ultimately a matter of preference and depends primarily on what you're building. However, there are two simple ways to begin to organize your project: structural and kanban method.

Structural project management

Here is an example of the Project Management Board I created to write and publish this book. This Project Management Board had Key Objectives and Task Lists entered throughout the course of the production of the book, from outlining to writing, to editing, packaging, marketing, and selling.

As you can see, the lists created inside Trello reflect a specific, structural component to my project (i.e. the Front Matter of the book, the Back Matter of the book, Transcriptions, etc.). This allowed me to segment the work to be done based on a collection of Key Objectives, all of which needed to be completed in order to finish and ship this book.

Within each list are cards that represent Key Objectives. Inside each Key Objective is a fully developed Task List, which allowed me to assign tasks that could be accomplished in 60 minutes or less.

Structural project management is a simple way to begin work on your project and great for more straight forward projects with less variables.

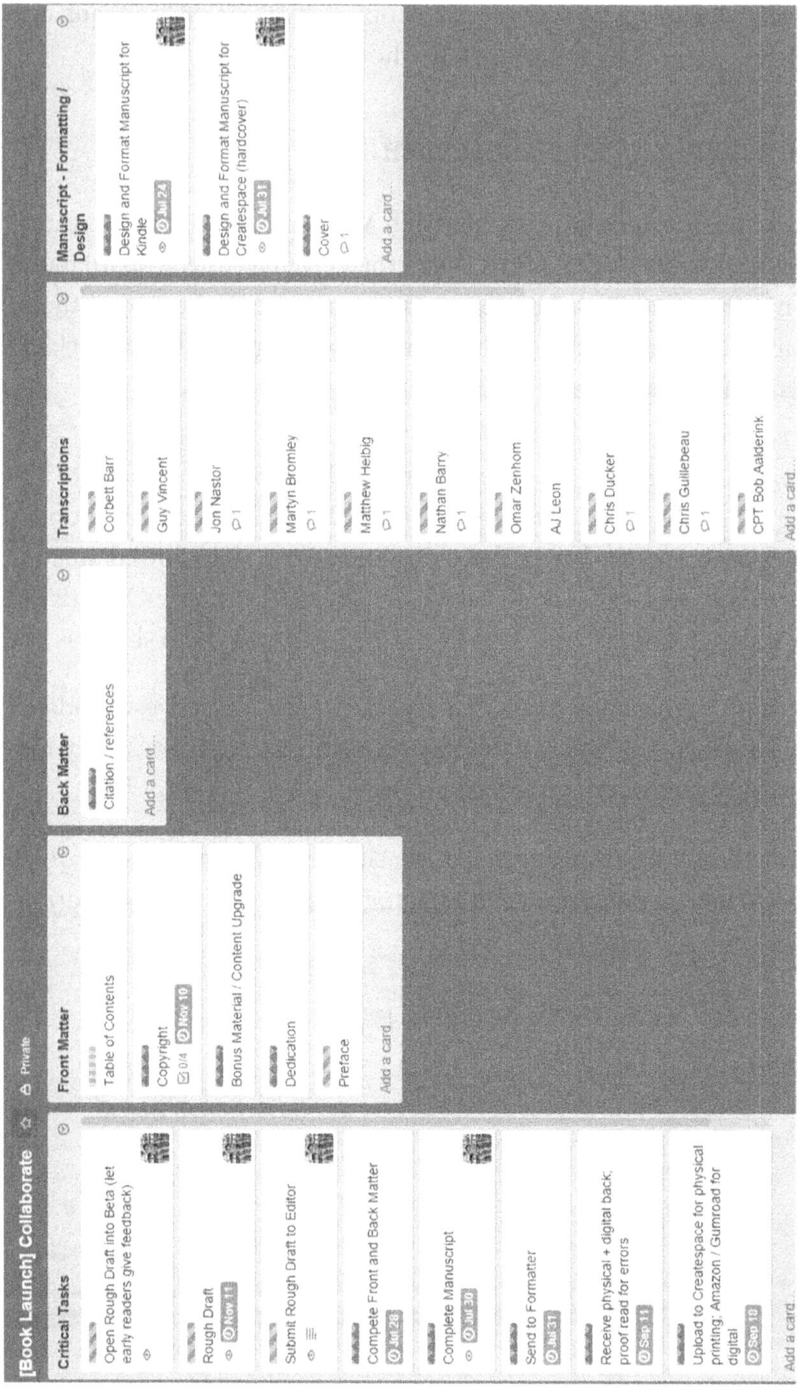
[Book Launch] Collaborate
Private
Critical Tasks
Open Rough Draft into Beta (let early readers give feedback)
Rough Draft
Submit Rough Draft to Editor
Compete Front and Back Matter
Complete Manuscript
Send to Formatter
Receive physical + digital back; proof read for errors
Upload to Createspace for physical printing; Amazon / Gumroad for digital
Add a card...
Front Matter
Table of Contents
Copyright
Bonus Material / Content Upgrade
Dedication
Preface
Add a card...
Back Matter
Citation / references
Add a card...
Transcriptions
Corbett Barr
Guy Vincent
Jon Nastor
Martyn Bromley
Matthew Helbig
Nathan Barry
Omar Zenhom
AJ Leon
Chris Ducker
Chris Guillebeau
CPT Bob Aalderink
Add a card...
Manuscript - Formatting / Design
Design and Format Manuscript for Kindle
Design and Format Manuscript for Createspace (hardcover)
Cover
Add a card...

Kanban project management

"Kanban is a visual signal that's used to trigger an action. The word kanban is Japanese and roughly translated means 'card you can see.' Toyota introduced and refined the use of kanban in a relay system to standardize the flow of parts in their just-in-time (JIT) production lines in the 1950s." —Techtarget.com[1]

Kanban is organized using a flow process, where Tasks are moved across a set of columns (lists) along a board as they progress: Backlog, To Do, In Process, Tested, Complete (or some variation of this flow). A core function of making Kanban work is making sure no single Task stays in a single column for too long. The goal is progress, and that means making sure every Task or Key Objective moves across the board in a timely fashion.

The great part about Kanban is that it's easy to apply to Trello, using Trello lists as the columns of development (e.g. This is very common for engineering work, where releasing reliable code is necessary for a software company to continue working correctly).

Publishizer.com on project management

Guy Vincent on how he is collaboratively building Publishizer.com using Trello:

"First, it's important to make the goal, and the process for achieving it, clear. I personally achieve this through writing, letting it all flow out in freeform for however long it takes to get clarification on my thinking process by putting it to paper. Once I know what I want to achieve, then I can develop the plan. As I draft out the outline of the plan, I am able to get clarity on the steps necessary to make it happen. Once I know the steps involved, I turn them into cards in Trello, and assign those cards and task lists to whoever it is that needs to execute them.

As the lead on the project, I am ultimately accountable for making sure that these tasks get accomplished on time and to standard."

Step 6. Define the Critical-Path

"If the maximum time available for a job equals its duration the job is called critical. A delay in a critical job will cause a comparable delay in the project completion time...If a project does contain critical jobs, then it also contains at least one contiguous path of critical jobs through the project diagram from origin to terminus. Such a path is called a critical-path." —Critical-Path Planning and Scheduling[2]

The Critical-Path is the sequence of Key Objectives (and, therefore, individual Tasks) that must be completed in sequential order or the entire project will be delayed. For example, if you're selling a book, writing the book is a Critical-Path item; you must write a book before you can edit it, and you must edit a book before you format it, and you must format a book before you print and ship it. In order for the final book to reach the hands of your happy reader, these events must take place in this order. This means writing becomes a Critical-Path Key Objective.

In comparision, things like press releases, podcast interviews, and blog posts may be Key Objectives, but because they can be completed at any point during the project, they are not Critical-Path Key Objectives.

The point of Critical-Path items is that these items cannot be completed until something before them is completed. In this way you get a very clear idea of what is of the highest priority and can focus on these Tasks and Key Objectives from the start.

You can discover the Critical-Path of your project by asking the following questions. Use the space below to outline your answers:

What must be accomplished for the user to receive your product and be 100% satisfied?

What is absolutely necessary to do or create to deliver on our promise to our customer?

Anything that is not absolutely necessary for your project should be put aside at first.

It's important to remember that, there is always at least one Critical-Path, but for multi-faceted projects, there may be several. For example, your marketing and sales campaign is most likely independent of your product development, which means there will be a unique Critical-Path for both processes. This means you need to identify the Critical-Path for product development and the Critical-Path for marketing and sales.

How to mark the Critical-Path in your workflow

Knowing the Critical-Path is essential for the success of your project. This requires that you mark Critical-Path items so all collaborators are aware of the highest-priority items. There are two simple ways to mark the Critical-Path in your workflow.

First, you can do so by creating a unique Critical Task List of Key Objectives. All Key Objective cards would then be moved into this list, and color-coded based on its status (green = complete, orange = in progress, red = not started). This is what I did for this book:

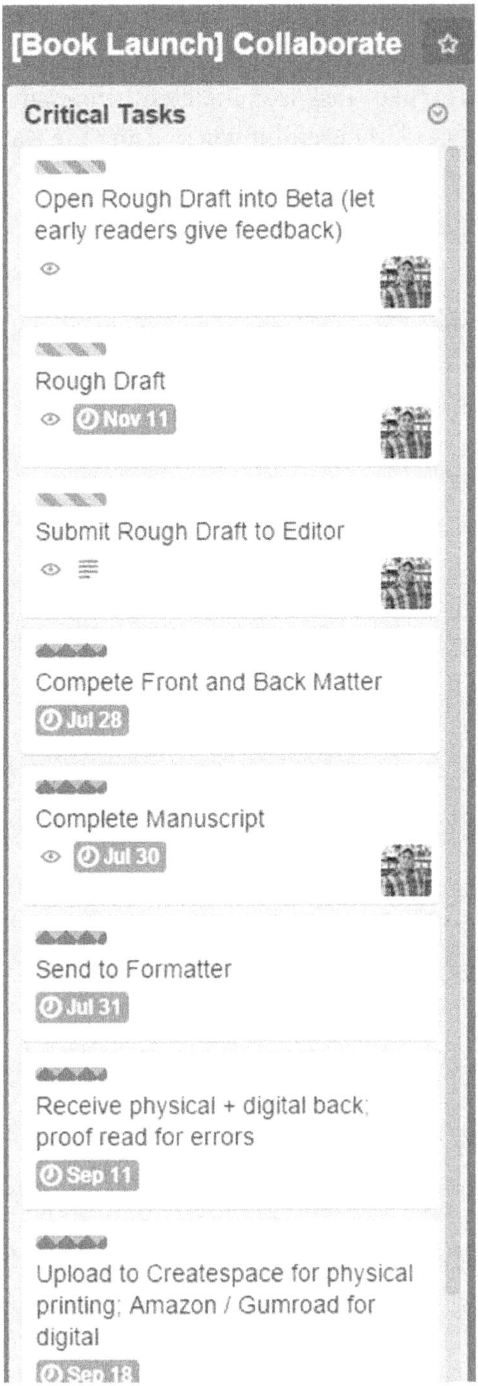
[Book Launch] Collaborate
Critical Tasks
Open Rough Draft into Beta (let early readers give feedback)
Rough Draft
Nov 11
Submit Rough Draft to Editor
Compete Front and Back Matter
Jul 28
Complete Manuscript
Jul 30
Send to Formatter
Jul 31
Receive physical + digital back; proof read for errors
Sep 11
Upload to Createspace for physical printing; Amazon / Gumroad for digital
Sep 18

Another way is to use specific labels or color-coding to identify Critical-Path Tasks. This would mean labeling items that cannot be completed until another particular Task is completed beforehand with the same color. This is particularly useful if you're using the Kanban method of Project Management, as you can see at a glance what string of items need to be completed in which order (otherwise, a Kanban board can become unruly with a lot of Key Objectives).

Here's an example:

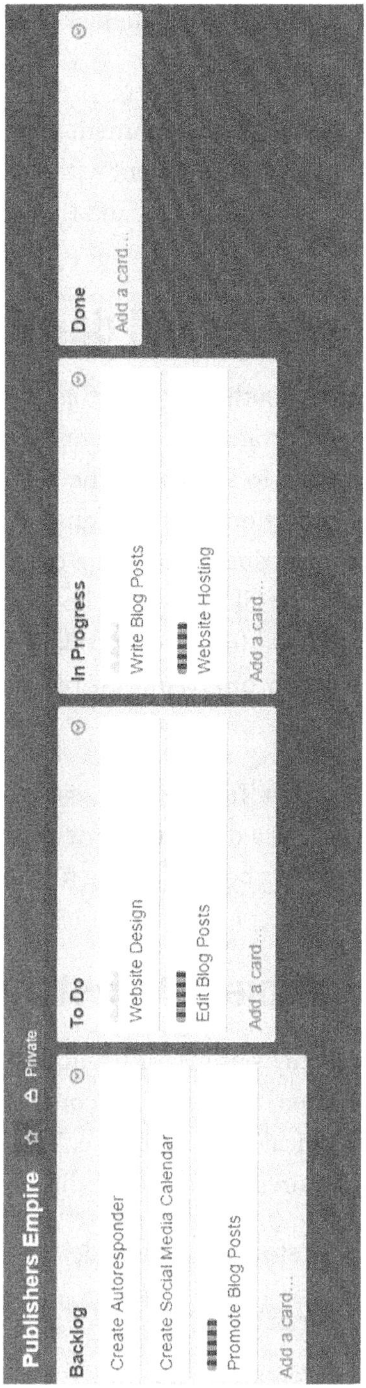
Publishers Empire
Private
Backlog
Create Autoresponder
Create Social Media Calendar
Promote Blog Posts
Add a card...
To Do
Website Design
Edit Blog Posts
Add a card...
In Progress
Write Blog Posts
Website Hosting
Add a card...
Done
Add a card...

I use Trello's label feature to color code tasks, with each color representing a Critical-Path sequence.

Either type of Critical-Path item assignment works, so try out both to see which works for you (and experiment with others if you find something more appropriate to your project and the tools you're using).

Step 7. Assign tasks and due dates

Defining Key Objectives, outlining your Task List, and determining the Critical-Path are important, but none of it matters if Tasks aren't accomplished on time and to standard. The best way to ensure fluid, fast, and effective collaboration is by assigning each Task to a collaborator and setting a specific due date for the completion of each Task. Adding time constraints for all Tasks will allow you to more accurately gauge your timeline and will force every collaborator to take the project seriously—after all, no one wants to be the person holding up the project.

At this point, go back to your Task List and assign an individual collaborator to each Task as well as a due date. Review assigned Tasks and due dates with your collaborators before moving forward.

Step 8. Define Project Milestones

A Project Milestone is any significant event that occurs during your collaboration and is often the result of completing a series of Key Objectives within a Critical-Path sequence. The completion of every Project Milestone is required to finish and ship your project.

Examples of Project Milestones may include:

1. Completing your Sales Page
2. Completing presentation slides for your live webinar

3. Completing your sales funnel (web pages are up and operational)

Project Milestones may also be time based:

1. Halfway through the project (based on projected ship date)
2. 2 weeks left
3. 1 week left
4. Launch day

The purpose of defining Project Milestones is twofold:

1. To give collaborators a reference point for project completion
2. To motivate and energize your team periodically throughout the process

It's tough to keep up a high pace of production if a project lasts more than two weeks. By establishing Project Milestones, you can be sure to get additional effort out of your team prior to a deadline. This is why I recommend defining at least one Project Milestone per two weeks of estimated work (with the time estimation based on the completion date and individual due dates for Tasks above). Project Milestones should be established before moving forward.

Use the space below to set your project Project Milestones:

Step 9. Create a project timeline

At this point, you have everything you need to establish a timeline for your entire project. Take everything you've done in this section and make sure there is a clear, chronological progression of the entire project from start to finish.

Spend 30-60 minutes to review the timeline with your collaborators. Make sure each team member understands and agrees to the timeline and that all due dates are reasonable. This is your last chance to make sure you haven't overestimated or underestimated your ability to complete any particular aspect of your project. Conduct this review now before moving forward.

Collaborative Standard Operating Procedures

"First and foremost, the single biggest mistake that I see most people who run online businesses make is the fact that they don't have their SOP's in place. And it is a major issue because when someone leaves or when someone has to be replaced or the ball is dropped somehow, your operation can hit the fan because there is no guiding light, no rules or instructions to fall back on."—Chris Ducker, CEO of Virtual Staff Finder

A Standard Operating Procedure is a term used in the U.S. Military to define and outline the execution of any activity in the form of a step-by-step process. This ensures that no matter who is involved or what experience level they have, the same steps are taken and consistent results are attainable.

In combat, an SOP can be the difference between life or death. In creative collaboration, it's the difference between working rapidly, efficiently, and enjoyably, or your project dismantling along the way because the individuals involved weren't clear on what to do or how to do it.

While SOPs in the U.S. Military are often incredibly detailed (many of them hundreds of pages long) the Standard Operating Procedures you want to establish for your collaboration should be simple and focused on core principles that guide your collaborative work.

Here are the most important areas your SOP should cover:

Task Ownership

How do we know who is responsible for which tasks?

When you outline your collaborative project, you'll find that there are dozens of tasks that need to be completed in order to deliver your product on time and to standard. In a collaborative project, there are usually multiple tasks being worked on simultaneously. The only way to efficiently manage this, especially for a small team, is to assign one person Task Ownership over each unique Task. Every Task should also have a completion date or due date assigned to it individually.

Why Task Ownership

The combination of assigning one person ownership over a task, and identifying a ship date for said task, is so that you, as the leader of the collaborative project, can manage the project effortlessly. Instead of scrambling to see who needs to do what at any given time, Task Ownership allows the Lead Collaborator the ability to step back and view the project from a 10,000 foot perspective. This allows for better decision making and faster, more efficient work (nobody is confused as to what they are responsible for delivering or when). Further, identifying one particular owner with a corresponding ship date takes stress off of the entire group. This leads to better, more enjoyable work.

How to assign Task Ownership

Below is an example of assigning Task Ownership using Trello as your project management platform:

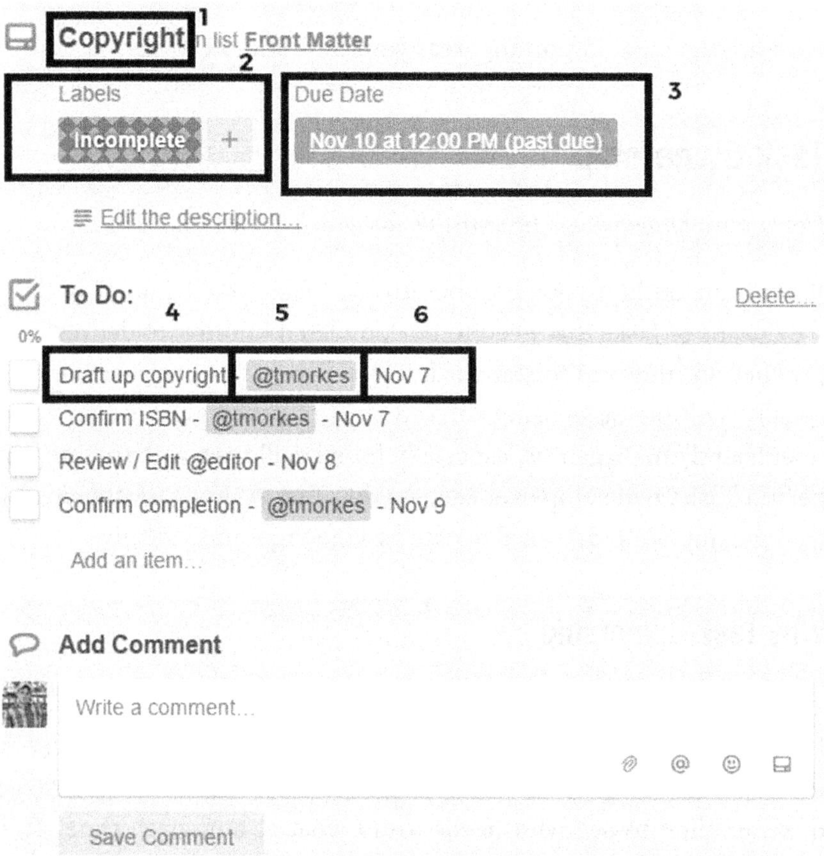

The numbers refer to the following:

1. Title of the Key Objective
2. Label to indicate status

3. Due date for Key Objective to be complete
4. Task List item description
5. Task List item assignment (this is assigning the person responsible for the Task)
6. Task List item due date (the due date for individual Task completion within a Key Objective)

Regardless of the platform you use, you should make sure it is clear who is responsible for each task, and have an assigned due date for that task. The person assigned the Task should understand the requirements for Task as well as the corresponding due date, and acknowledge Task Ownership in written format to the Lead Collaborator (via email, Slack, internal communication tools inside your project management tool, etc.—more communication standards later).

Item Control

Who is currently working on, and responsible for, this item?

More than likely, there will come a time when you need to be clear about who is working on what item so that no one else interferes with the Task being accomplished. Examples might include editing; it doesn't make sense for everyone to edit an offline document at once. This could result in people overwriting one another's work, thereby creating more work for the entire team. This slows progress and can cause conflict.

Before you set to work, make sure you identify when an item (document, file, etc.) requires Item Control. Examples might include:

1. The main document or manuscript
2. The website or webpage design template
3. Any document or file undergoing editing

4. Outreach or cold calling / emailing

If an item is marked as Item Control, there should only be one person assigned to the item and responsible for it; no one else should touch this item until the person assigned has completed his work and reassigned it to someone else.

Why Item Control

Item Control forces both accountability and efficiency on you and your collaborators. No person wants to be the one holding things up. When you clearly assign someone as the person currently responsibility for an important item, it's easier to track and manage that person and the item itself. By assigning Item Control, you will reduce ambiguity and uncertainty among collaborators.

Further, practicing Item Control reduces waste. This is especially relevant in remote collaborations where digital documents can be sent back and forth between parties and it very quickly becomes difficult to recognize the most updated version. In the cases where you're using a collaborative document, such as Google Docs, there is also the possibility of sync issues, where the document won't properly save and the other person won't receive the most updated file. Again, practicing Item Control can reduce the risk of errors by making it clear when a document or other item is in someone else's possession.

How to assign Item Control

Below is an example of assigning Item Control to a single person within Trello:

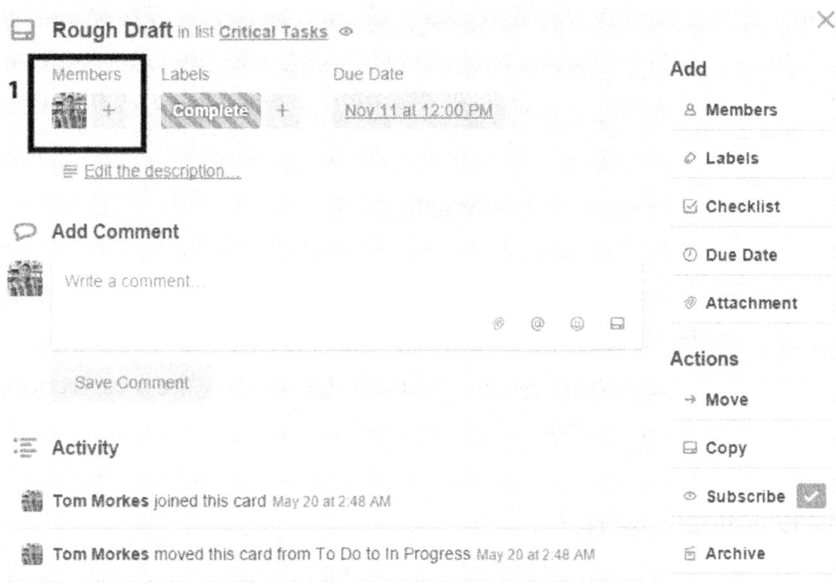

The numbers refer to the following:

1. The person assigned Item Control to this particular item (Rough Draft).

Trello allows you to assign "Members" to an individual card. A simple way to maintain Item Control is to make sure each card has no more than one assigned person who is solely responsible for it for as long as he or she is assigned to it. Once complete, the assigned person should assign the next party responsible and update the card (either by updating the label, Task List, or moving the card to another list inside Trello to indicate the item status).

Accountability

How do we keep ourselves and each other accountable?

When it comes to collaboration, especially remote collaboration for a digital product, accountability is essential. This includes both personal accountability (*can I get this task done on time and to standard without it ruining my social or personal life?*) and project accountability (*how do I make sure all collaborators are executing on time and to standard?*).

The best way to ensure accountability is to:

1. Define Task Ownership
2. Monitor Item Control
3. Conduct weekly Azimuth Checks (we'll cover the next section: "Staying on Track").

Why accountability?

Reg Seeton is a business coach and consultant who works with international teams on collaborative, remote projects. Here's Seeton's take on accountability:

"Accountability is a necessity. I look at it the same way as a car. You can't drive a car without an engine. You can't run a successful business or execute targets within a project without holding yourself accountable. Accountability is the fuel that gets you to where you need to be from beginning to end. I separate accountability from organization and discipline, and mentally streamline each so they're each individual processes that require different solutions. Accountability leads to discipline which leads to better organization," says Seeton.

"Above all, accountability is a deep, personal commitment with yourself. You can't be accountable unless you want to be that type of person or professional. If you truly want to be accountable, you can transform your life or career."

Corbett Barr on the importance of SOPs

Corbett Barr is the founder and CEO of Fizzle.co, a leading online business training program and community. He built Fizzle.co collaboratively with two of his good friends. The entire project, from start to finish, was built remotely, making reliable Standard Operating Procedures essential to their success:

"I think the most important thing is to design what I call the operating system of the business. So, just like your phone has a set of operating system instructions, that basically tell the phone how to operate, you, as a leader, need to create an operating system for the team. And that operating system is going to evolve over time, and it's going to look different depending on what your scenario is, and whether or not people are employees or contractors and all that sort of stuff. The most important thing is to realize that if you don't set some sort of operating system at the outset then something's going to happen and the thing that becomes the operating system, the de facto operating system, may be good or it may be bad."

The 80/20 Principle for collaboration

In the early 20th century, Vilfredo Pareto, an Italian engineer, sociologist and economist, measured the distribution of land throughout Italy. He observed that 80% of the land was owned by 20% of the population. Remarkably, he found this same type of power law distribution across various domains, from sociology to economics to science. His observations later became known as the Pareto principle, or the 80-20 rule, which states that, typically, 20% of causes create 80% of effects, and vice versa.

When we apply this to the domain of collaboration and online business, we find a few key efforts will create the majority of our positive results.

The following questions will help you get clarity on the 20% of effort that will lead to 80% of the results:

The 80/20 Principle and collaboration:

Focus	Questions	Answer
80/20 Principle and collaboration	What amount of meetings are necessary each week to keep everyone on track and working? If we doubled the amount of meetings, what would happen? If we cut the total number of meetings in half, what would happen?	
	What is the simplest way for us to communicate?	
	What could double the speed of our collaboration? What could triple it? What could make it move 10x faster?	
	What single thing about collaborating is the most enjoyable and rewarding? How do we maximize this?	

Staying on track

The enemy of every collaborative project is time decay.

Time decay is a term used in options trading (in real estate or stocks). It refers to the fact that, as time goes by, an option contract loses value. Why? Because every option has an expiration date. The closer you get to expiration, the less chance that your option will create any additional value beyond what it currently has.

Collaboration is no different.

I believe the single greatest threat to collaboration is time decay: if a project takes too long, you will inevitably run out of one of the following:

1. Money (even if you're bootstrapping, taking too long will drain your wallet)
2. Energy (moving so slowly that collaborators lose interest)
3. Time (people get busy, things come up, new and better opportunities will present themselves almost every day)

So if time decay is the greatest threat, speed is your best friend.

As the leader of a collaborative project, it's your responsibility to make sure you and your collaborators are completing Tasks and Key Objectives on time and to standard, and that the entire project is moving toward your desired end-state daily.

Here are some ways to maintain progress and move fast (without sacrificing quality):

#1. Stay in constant communication

Collaborative success is directly correlated to the quality and quantity of team communication. In other words, the more often you communicate with your collaborators, the more likely you're going to finish and ship on time. The more likely you are to finish and ship on time, the greater your chances of success.

The best way to ensure progress is to stay in daily communication with your collaborators.

Good news: it's never been easier to connect with anyone in the world almost instantly. Here are just a few of the incredible tools that are at your disposal to stay on track and on target.

Slack

Slack is a real-time messaging application that seamlessly integrates across devices. While there are other real-time messaging apps out there, Slack is simple to learn, intuitive to use, and robust; there are dozens of integrations that make Slack incredibly powerful, from video conference calls to screen sharing, to the simple way you can share Google Drive documents with collaborators.

You can find slack at www.slack.com

Skype

Skype is a free Voice Over Internet Protocol (VOIP) application that lets you make calls to anyone in the world on Skype for free (and to landlines and cell phones for a price). Skype allows group calling and screen sharing, making it great for communication.

You can find Skype at www.skype.com

Google Hangouts

Google Hangouts is a lot like Skype: free and easy to use. You can do group calls, screen sharing, and easily share documents during live calls.

You can find Google Hangouts at www.hangouts.google.com

#2. Conduct weekly Azimuth Checks

One of the first skills every soldier in the U.S. Army learns is land navigation. That is, the act of finding your way to some location with nothing more than a map, a compass, and a grid coordinate. The challenge with land navigation is twofold. First, you need to figure out where you are. This requires triangulation (a technique I won't get into here).

Second, after you figure out where you are, you need to figure out how to get to your destination.

Believe it or not, even after you've placed a dot on a map, actually finding it can be quite difficult. Once you start moving, it's not uncommon to wind up completely turned around. The only way to make sure you stay on track is to do periodic azimuth checks. An azimuth check is the process of taking a pause during your movement over terrain to figure out exactly where you are in relation to your objective (the point on the map you want to reach).

A good project manager incorporates Azimuth Checks into the product development process. Here's how to conduct your own Azimuth Checks:

How to conduct an Azimuth Check

Step 1. Schedule consistent meetings

At the outset of your project, you should establish dates and times to conduct Azimuth Checks. These can be daily, weekly, or monthly, and can also be based on achieving certain Key Objectives or Project Milestones. You can also conduct spur of the moment Azimuth Checks in the case of new information entering the equation.

I recommend setting at least one consistent, weekly date and time as a check-in with your collaborators. No collaborator should miss this meeting.

Step 2. Start with a 5 minute individual task summary

Have each collaborator do a brief overview of Task and Key Objectives completed the previous week, as well as what they're working on this week.

Step 3. Conduct 15 minute project overview

The Lead Collaborator should do a brief overview of what's been accomplished over the course of the last two weeks, and what the next two weeks should bring. This gives everyone a better view of the project and how much progress you've made. Focus on Task and Key Objective accomplishment (both what has been completed and what needs to be completed). Make sure all collaborators are aware of Task Ownership and Item Control when and where appropriate.

Step 4. Avoid brainstorming and debating

Weekly meetings become pointless if they devolve into brainstorming sessions or debates. In situations where brainstorming is necessary, a different type of meeting should be organized, or it should be handled through a one-on-one call.

#3. Track and share completion and successes

Nobody likes working in ambiguity. The inherent nature of entrepreneurship is situational uncertainty; you can't know what is going to happen with 100% certainty. You do not want to add to this uncertainty by limiting communication, by forgetting to review the project purpose (and progress) on a regular basis with your team, or by forgetting to share individual accomplishments with the whole team. By sharing individual accomplishments and project progress, team morale and motivation will increase.

I've found one of the best ways to encourage and motivate your collaborators is to have a visual, transparent tracker of success. You can track this within your project management software (having a "Done" list in Trello, or by simply labeling items "Complete"), or you can manage a separate document, such as a Hackpad document that solely tracks Key Objective accomplishment. Always devote at least five minutes during your weekly Azimuth Checks to share these statistics with the whole team, and do your best to recognize those who are accomplishing Tasks and Key Objectives.

#4. Embrace Project Milestones

The success or failure of a project comes down to completing Tasks, Key Objectives, and, ultimately, Critical-Path items on time and to standard. Due dates of all Tasks, Key Objectives, and Critical-Path items should be monitored by the Lead Collaborator. If a Project Milestone is missed, it is up to the Lead Collaborator to get his or her team back on track.

As Project Milestones are completed, the Lead Collaborator should make a point to revisit the project with all collaborators, both to celebrate the accomplishment of a new Project Milestone, as well as review next steps in the project.

Azimuth Check

The key to successful collaboration is progress. To maintain progress, stay in constant communication with your teammates, adhere to your established timeline, and hold one another accountable to Task and Key Objective completion. Remember that 20% of your efforts create 80% of your results. Don't waste time on tertiary activities—stick to what is important. And of course, always celebrate your wins.

Take a short break here to take notes or add your thoughts below before moving onto the next Milestone:

PHASE 4

LAUNCH

Milestone 11: Create Your Sales Funnel

Milestone 12: Pre-Sell Your Product

Milestone purpose

To conduct final preparation before your collaborative launch.

Milestone checklist

- ☐ Understand what makes people buy
- ☐ Build your sales funnel
- ☐ Begin marketing

MILESTONE 11

CREATE YOUR SALES FUNNEL

Why does it seem like some companies are able to seduce customers into buying everything they make, while others seem to completely miss the mark? The most ubiquitous consumer product example might be Apple. It's not uncommon for Apple fans to line up for days, sometimes even weeks, to buy their new products [1] (even when the new product doesn't work right).[2]

What is it that companies like Apple do to create such captivating, not to mention lucrative, launches? More importantly, can small collaborative teams mimic the same results on a budget?

In this Milestone, we'll cover these questions and more as we move into the launch phase of your digital product launch.

Psychological triggers that make people buy

Jeff Goins is the bestselling author of *The Art of Work*, the brains behind a newsletter for writers with more than 100,000 readers, and someone who has mastered the art of the online launch (his last book was a USA Today bestseller because of how he catalyzed his audience to buy on launch day).

According to Goins, there are four primary factors to get someone to buy your product or service.[3] They are:

1. Anticipation
2. Generosity
3. Urgency
4. Scarcity

I would add a fifth item to this list: Perceived Value

Perceived Value is crucial in order to market and price your product at a premium.

In the following section, we'll analyze each factor and show you ways to incorporate it into your product launch.

#1. Anticipation

J.J. Abrams is a writer, director, and producer, famous for blockbuster television shows like *Lost* and major motion pictures like *Star Wars: Episode VII.*

In a 2007 TED talk, Abrams delivered a presentation exploring the topic of mystery. During the presentation, Abram tells the story of a gift his grandfather gave him, a small cardboard box titled *Tannen's Mystery Magic Box*. Abram has held onto this box for decades, and it sits unopened on his bookshelf today. The reason, he explains, is that sometimes mystery is more important than knowledge.

The closed box, for Abram, "represents infinite possibility; it represents hope; it represents potential."[4]

In reality, every unopened door, every unknown path, every yet-to-be-released product represents the same thing: potential. And the desire to unleash this potential is what Abrams so eloquently describes as *anticipation*—that feeling you get when you aren't sure what's going to happen, but you believe it will be good.

With your launch, you want to build as much anticipation as possible before you open the cart (i.e. make the product readily available for purchase).

How a guaranteed $10,000 launch flopped

Nathan Barry is the founder of ConvertKit, an email marketing service for bloggers, the author of *Authority*, and a respected designer and product launch expert. Barry knows how to create anticipation for his product launches; in just 18 months, he earned more than $300,000 from digital product launches.

However, not all of his launches have been five or six figure successes.

Back in 2013, Barry was preparing a workshop for web application designers. At this point, Barry had built an email list of 5,000 designers. He planned to price the workshop at $400 with an attendance cap of 25 seats. According to Barry, "it was going to be an easy $10,000. In fact, I remember thinking, 'with an email list of 5,000, how hard can it be to sell 25 seats?'"

Barry sent his list the email about the new workshop and waited for sales to roll in...

Nothing.

Barry forgot an essential factor in generating sales at launch: anticipation.

How to build anticipation

"[most people] think about a product for a while before coming to a decision. So if you tell your audience about your product and then in the same email ask them to buy it, that won't result in many sales. Really, your goal should be to build up that anticipation and excitement before you give them an opportunity to buy. Use teaching and sharing to get them excited, and then say 'Want to buy it?' When they respond with 'Yes!' say, 'Cool. You can next Tuesday.' In short you want them to decide whether or not they are going to buy, before you give them an opportunity to buy."—Nathan Barry, CEO of ConvertKit.com[5]

Learning from Barry's flop (and subsequent quarter million in successful launches), here's what you can do to build anticipation for your launch:

1. Start by teaching; provide relevant, useful content for your readers before you mention your product
2. Hint at your product; mention in one of your educational messages that you're building something that could help your prospective customer achieve X (whatever problem you're solving—refer to your one page business model)
3. Tease; launch the product, but with no way to buy. Instead, let people know the exact date and time the cart will open
4. Finally, open the cart, answering common objectives prospective customers might have about your product or service

Use the following space to outline ways you can build anticipation for your launch:

#2. Generosity

Robert Cialdini is the bestselling author of *Influence*, a seminal book on influence and persuasion in the world of marketing and sales. In *Influence*, Cialdini explores six principles of influence—things that lead people, often irrationally, to make choices (in this case, buy products or services).

According to Cialdini, one of the most powerful principles is reciprocity, or what happens when someone gives you a gift. Giving is so powerful because "we are obligated to the future repayment of favors, gifts, invitations, and the like. So typical is it for indebtedness to accompany the receipt of such things that a term like 'much obliged' has become a synonym for 'thank you,' not only in the English language but in others as well."[6]

Cialdini explains that one of the primary factors in why giving elicits such a strong response is because of our fear of being perceived as ungenerous:

"Because there is general distaste for those who take and make no effort to give in return, we will often go to great lengths to avoid being considered one of their number."

The question is, how do you take advantage of the rule of reciprocity to increase sales of your product at launch, while still doing everything with integrity?

How to Leverage Generosity for Your Launch

The simplest way to leverage the law of reciprocity is to give away relevant, helpful information to your audience prior to launching your product. The beauty of digital product launches is that information is cheaper than ever to distribute (close to zero marginal cost), yet that doesn't stop it from having an immense amount of value for the consumer if it's relevant and useful.

Referring back to building anticipation, look for ways you can include free guides, workbooks, or additional digital products into your pre-launch marketing. Examples may include:

1. Bonus PDF
2. Free eBook
3. Swipe File (a collection of resources pulled together in a particular topic)
4. Template
5. Cheat Sheet
6. Free webinar

The best gift will be something relevant and useful to your audience, so refer back to your one page business model to see if there's anything that could add more value to your ideal customer and the problem he or she is dealing with.

Use the following space to outline how you can use generosity in your launch:

#3. Urgency

Urgency is the process of getting people to act now, not later. For product launches, we want our potential customers to buy now, on launch day, not wait until some vague time in the future.

How to increase urgency

According to Nathan Barry,[7] there are three ways to increase urgency:

1. Discount the price
2. Add a bonus
3. Limit sales

#1. Discount the price

Discounting your price is arguably the easiest way to increase urgency, but it is also potentially dangerous. You need to find a way to discount your price without losing profit. Further, you don't want to devalue your product or service by offering too steep a discount.

If you intend to discount the price of your product, make sure you have done the math to define your minimum profitable price (i.e. after all expenses, is this still worth selling at this price?), as well as clearly articulated to your potential customer how long the discount will be available. You can compound the effect of this technique by promising that the price will never again be this low, and that any purchase is "grandfathered in" if you decide to raise prices later (great for subscription or membership services).

#2. Add a bonus

I believe bonuses are the single best way to increase the value of a product. Bonuses can add an incredible amount of perceived value without diminishing the value of your original product, and there is no threat of losing profit margin, as a well constructed bonus can command a higher price for the entire package.

However, in order to leverage bonuses to increase urgency, they must be time-bound and limited. This is the major hurdle with bonuses—worthwhile bonuses take time, money, and energy to build, so making them exclusive to pre-orders or early adopters means only a few people will get access to them.

You will need to consider what's a worthwhile bonus for your particular audience and decide if the investment will be worth your projected return. In other words—will this bonus increase total sales? One way to test this out is by incrementally adding bonuses during your launch sequence.

Example:

Day 1 bonus: MP3 question-and-answer recording

Day 2 bonus: Video interviews with leading experts

Day 3 bonus: Extra checklists, swipe copy, and more

The questions you want to ask as you develop a bonus:

"does this improve the function of the original product or service? Does it make it easier to implement the product or service? Will this improve the results of the customer if he or she uses it in conjunction with the original product or service?"

A "yes" to any of the above makes for a worthwhile bonus.

#3. Limit sales

Another simple way to increase urgency is by limiting how many people can purchase your product. Pay attention to just about any online product launch and you'll see this technique used. If you're launching to 1,000 people, but you only make 10 slots available—and you let your audience know this—you will encourage fence-sitters (those who aren't sure whether to buy now or later) to buy now. The fear of loss is a very powerful motivator, and limiting sales increases this fear.

Use the following space to outline how you can create urgency with your launch:

Questions to discuss with your collaborators

Focus	Questions	Answer
How to increase urgency for our product launch	What is our minimum break even price? Can we discount by 10% (or 20%) and still make a profit?	
	What are additional items that would add to the utility of our product? Can we include them without increasing marginal cost?	
	How big is our combined reach? Does it benefit us to limit total sales for version 1.0?	

#4. Scarcity

Scarcity, like urgency, is a psychological trigger that compels people to buy now, not later. However, scarcity has another positive side-effect for product creators: people value things that are perceived to be more rare.

According to a study from the International Journal of Research in Marketing (Gierl & Huettl, 2010), "signals of scarcity due to high demand result in more favorable product evaluations" specifically when dealing with "conspicuous" consumer products (i.e. things other people can see you use, like an iPhone).[8]

Cookies in a jar

In 1975, an experiment was conducted to determine if scarcity had an impact on the perception of value. Researchers Worchel, Lee, and Adewole, used cookies in a jar; sometimes they were in abundant supply, sometimes in scarce supply, with different stories about why they were abundant, why they were scarce, and why they were changing between the two.

The results were generally what you might expect: cookies in scarce supply were more desireable than cookies in abundant supply. When cookies went from abundant to scarce, they were perceived to be more valuable (and were the most valuable when scarcity was due to high demand, as opposed to by accident). Finally, and most surprisingly, cookies that were consistently abundant had higher value than those which were scarce and became abundant.[9]

In other words, if you use scarcity, make sure you start more abundantly and move toward more scarcity, not the other way around.

How to increase scarcity

There are a number of takeaways from this research.

Step 1. Limit total sales of your product

We mentioned this as a compelling way to increase urgency. It also works to increase scarcity.

Step 2. Increase the price of your product over time

If you're launching your first iteration of a product or service, let people know the price will go up from here. According to the study above, scarcity increases value when the item becomes more scarce over time. Conversely, perceived value drops if the product becomes less scarce over time, more so than if it simply stays abundant. In other words, make sure you are making your products more scarce over time, and never go the opposite way (scarcity to abundance destroys perceived value).

Step 3. Use a countdown timer / meter

Specifically, include a ticker that shows total units that are left (e.g. 2 of 10 remaining!), or time until sale ends (e.g. 10 minutes remaining!). Simple reminders like this will not only create urgency, but will remind consumers that the product is in high demand and short supply.

Use the following space to outline how you can use scarcity in your launch:

#5. Perceived value

Value is an interesting thing. While we might believe that humans rationally value products and services, nothing could be further from the truth. The reality is that modern marketing has perfected the art of increasing perceived value. Here's one great example (it may leave a bad taste in your mouth about brands, marketing, and sales in general):

"I once heard a talk given by the vice president of merchandising from a national chain of young women's clothing stores in which she deconstructed a particular display of T-shirts. 'We buy them in Sri Lanka for three dollars each,' she began. 'Then we bring them over here and sew in washing instructions in French and English—French on the front, English on the back. Notice we don't say the shirts are made in France.

But you can infer that if you like. Then we merchandise the hell out of them—we fold them just right on a tasteful tabletop display, and on the wall behind it we hang a huge, gorgeous photograph of a beautiful woman in an exotic locale wearing the shirt. We shoot it so it looks like a million bucks. Then we call it an Expedition T-shirt, and we sell it for thirty-seven dollars. And we sell a lot of them, too.'"—*Why We Buy* by Paco Underhill [10]

The author goes on to share his reaction to the presentation:

"It was the most depressing valuable lesson I've ever had."

How to increase perceived value

Besides increase urgency and scarcity, there are several things you can do to increase the perceived value of any product you bring to market.

Step 1. Share positive reviews

According to Bright Local's Consumer Survey in 2013, not only are more people searching for reviews online before making a purchase, but they need to read fewer reviews than ever before coming to a conclusion about your product or service.[11] This trend doesn't look set to change any time soon.

When it comes to presenting your product or service, you have the opportunity to structure how people perceive your work by sharing powerful, useful testimonials with your audience. Make sure the testimonials are honest, that they tackle a particular issue potential customers might have about buying your product (e.g. "it's the cheapest product on the market that does X"), and that they include images of the person giving the testimonial (because images increase credibility).[12]

Step 2. Get endorsements from celebrities

A celebrity endorsement is like a review, but from a well-known name in your niche. These types of endorsements are important because, like reviews, they can help people form quick, positive opinions about you. The right endorsement can make you look reliable, trustworthy, and successful.

Step 3. Price anchor

Price anchoring is a pricing technique that allows you to increase the perceived value of a product or service by placing it next to something similar, but more expensive. Price anchoring works for two reasons.

First, by putting your product or service next to a comparable, but more expensive product, yours looks inexpensive by comparison. This will make customers feel like they're getting a great deal.

Second, by positioning your product next to a higher-end competitor, you are subconsciously telling the customer that your product is comparable to the higher-end competitors. This is a very powerful technique if you're competing against major corporate incumbents (and just as important if you're launching a niche product but want to ensure people recognize the value of what you're creating).

Use the following space to outline how you can increase the perceived value of your launch:

Summary of psychological triggers to increase sales

The principles of influence, persuasion, marketing and sales are powerful things. It's important to note that, like any tool, they can be used for good or evil. While it's easy to push all these levers to full-throttle, if you want to build a legitimate business, it's important to act with integrity at all times. Use the following set of questions to discuss with your collaborators how you should incorporate these psychological triggers into your product launch:

Focus	Questions	Answer
Maintaining integrity in the sales process	If our potential customer knew the full story behind what we are offering, would they still pay asking price?	
	Is there anything we're leaving out that, if someone learned about, would influence their decision to buy?	
	Is our product legitimately helping people and improving their lives? What if it does not deliver on the promise?	

Defining the sales funnel

"The definition of the sales funnel (also known as a revenue funnel or sales process) refers to the buying process that companies lead customers through when purchasing products. A sales funnel is divided into several steps, which differ depending on the particular sales model." —Ringdna.com[13]

The concept of the sales funnel has been around for hundreds of years. But it's only been in the last 20 years that they've developed a new meaning, thanks to the internet and the proliferation of cheap technology. Modern internet sales funnels have helped hundreds of startups rapidly grow from nothing to millions (sometimes billions) in revenue (see: Uber, Airbnb, Slack, etc.). One of the most famous startup sales funnel models was created by Dave McClure, entrepreneur, angel investor, and the founder of the Silicon Valley-based incubator, 500 Startups. McClure's funnel is nicknamed the "pirate" model because of its acronym: AAARR.[14]

These five elements of the "pirate" sales funnel are: Acquisition, Activation, Retention, Referral, and Revenue.

> **Acquisition:** get someone to your site
>
> **Activation:** get this person to take action (free trial, newsletter subscription,etc.)
>
> **Retention:** get this person to come back to your site multiple times (coming back to use their free trial, coming back through your newsletter, etc.)
>
> **Referral:** get this person to spread the word, either directly or indirectly. For example: directly—word of mouth; indirectly—putting your logo on the software so when others see it, there's a chance they'll click on it.
>
> **Revenue:** get this person to buy something (upgrade to paid version of your software, buy your book, join your premium ecourse or training program, etc.)

Avoiding complexity in your sales funnel

As you can see, there are a lot of things to think about as you prepare to market and sell your product. Because there are hundreds of ways to build out your sales funnel, there are hundreds of ways to get it wrong.

In order to avoid building a sales funnel that doesn't work, it's important to remember that every sales funnel boils down to three steps:

1. Attracting your ideal customer
2. Engaging with your ideal customer in the way they prefer
3. Motivating your ideal customer to buy now, not later

If you miss any one of these steps, your launch won't work.

The truth is, most product launch failures are "user-error" failures. Many solopreneurs who fail to sell their product or service fail because they've spent their time and money on the wrong elements of the funnel. In order to avoid this same fate, you need to focus on the essential elements of your funnel, and only put your time and energy into activities with the highest return on investment.

That's where "The 1-1-1 Product Launch Method" comes in...

The 1-1-1 Product Launch Method

For a collaborative, digital product launch, we can streamline the sales funnel into three key activities, known as The 1-1-1 Product Launch Method. These are:

1. One Lead Generator
2. One Lead Capture Page
3. One Lead Conversion Process

By following The 1-1-1 Product Launch Method, you'll be able to cut out the fat and fluff of most online business advice and refine your product launch into something simple, intuitive, measurable, and most of all, effective.

Here's how to do it one step at a time:

1. One Lead Generator

A Lead Generator is the strategy and process you'll use to find your ideal customers and send them to your Lead Capture Page.

Here are just a few examples of online Lead Generators:

1. Guest blogging
2. Paid advertising
3. Social media
4. Current list / newsletter
5. Joint venture
6. Affiliates

There are hundreds of ways to drive customers to a website online. That also means there are hundreds of ways to mess up lead generation. While companies generating millions in revenue can test multiple processes, this is not an effective strategy for bootstrapped, collaborative projects. If time, money, and resources are limited, it doesn't make sense to try to drive traffic from a podcast, Facebook ads, content marketing, and affiliates all at the same time. Instead, you increase your chances of success by focusing on a single Lead Generator so you can properly test and measure it.

As you go through the process of creating your Lead Generator, remember the 80/20 rule—one process will inevitably create much better results than all the others.

"At any stage in a startup's lifecycle, one traction channel dominates in terms of customer acquisition."—*Traction* by Justin Mares[15]

Which Lead Generator should I start with?

The following chart is a reference point to help you get started:

Type	Difficulty	Effectiveness	Scalability	Ideal price of product
Guest blogging	Moderate	High	Low	Low
Paid advertising	High	Moderate	High	High
Social media	Low	Low	Moderate	Low / Moderate
Current list / newsletter	Moderate	High	Moderate	Moderate
Joint venture	High	Very High	Low	High
Affiliates	High	High	Moderate	Moderate / High

Use the chart above to brainstorm potential Lead Generators with your collaborators.

Use the space below to identify the single Lead Generator you will use for your launch:

Using guest blogging as your primary Lead Generator

"I think a lot of guest posts are complete failures. In order to prevent that from happening there are two things that you have to do.

1. the post has to be really good.
2. you need to have a free offer of some kind for the people who read that post.

So for example, I wrote a blog post for Smash magazine. It's about four thousand words long, entitled, 'How To Launch Anything.' At the end of that post, there's a link to a free email course that I created called 'Mastering Product Launches.' So, anyone who reads through the entire blog post gets to the end and I don't just say, 'Hey check this out,' I use the last paragraph or two to tie it in and say if you've gotten this far, you obviously care deeply about product launches, and you'll really want to really learn more about them. So I have this free course, go here, sign up.

It's really important to have that tie into the free offering. And so off that, I am getting a thousand email subscribers, off that one guest post. And part of that is because Smash magazine is a truly massive blog. But, you know, if I had just relied on having a link in my author bio or something, I don't think it would have worked out so well. So if you do guest posts, you have to make sure you have a strong offer. You can link to it well, and that's when things start to convert well, and you can see, you know, a hundred, five hundred email subscribers from a single guest post."—Nathan Barry, the founder of ConvertKit.com

2. One Lead Capture Page

All your efforts should guide people to one page. The purpose of this page is to do one thing: get the visitor to sign up to learn more or get more information. In the process, you capture their information (name and email address at a minimum) so you can follow up with them later (to eventually pitch and sell your product or service). In other words, the goal of the Lead Capture Page is to build a subscriber list (or equivalent).

Tools and software for Lead Capture

There are two elements you need to turn traffic (random internet passerbies) into subscribers:

1. A splash page
2. An Email Marketing Service (EMS)

While there are many options for splash page creation and lots of Email Marketing Services on the market, there are a few tools I recommend for bootstrappers and collaborative projects that can make the process fast, cheap, and generally painless.

Splash page

WordPress.org

WordPress is a popular blogging framework. You can customize the look of your website with Themes, many which are free or low cost ($25-$75). Creating a splash page in WordPress is as simple as creating a page inside your WordPress site and making sure it's set to landing page (no header, no distractions). Then simply add a call to action for people to optin to your list. This is one of the cheapest ways to get up and running.

Here's an example of a splash page built on wordpress. The buttons, when clicked, create an optin box to appear, requesting the visitors first name and email address. This allows me to add them to my Email Marketing Service and follow up with them later:

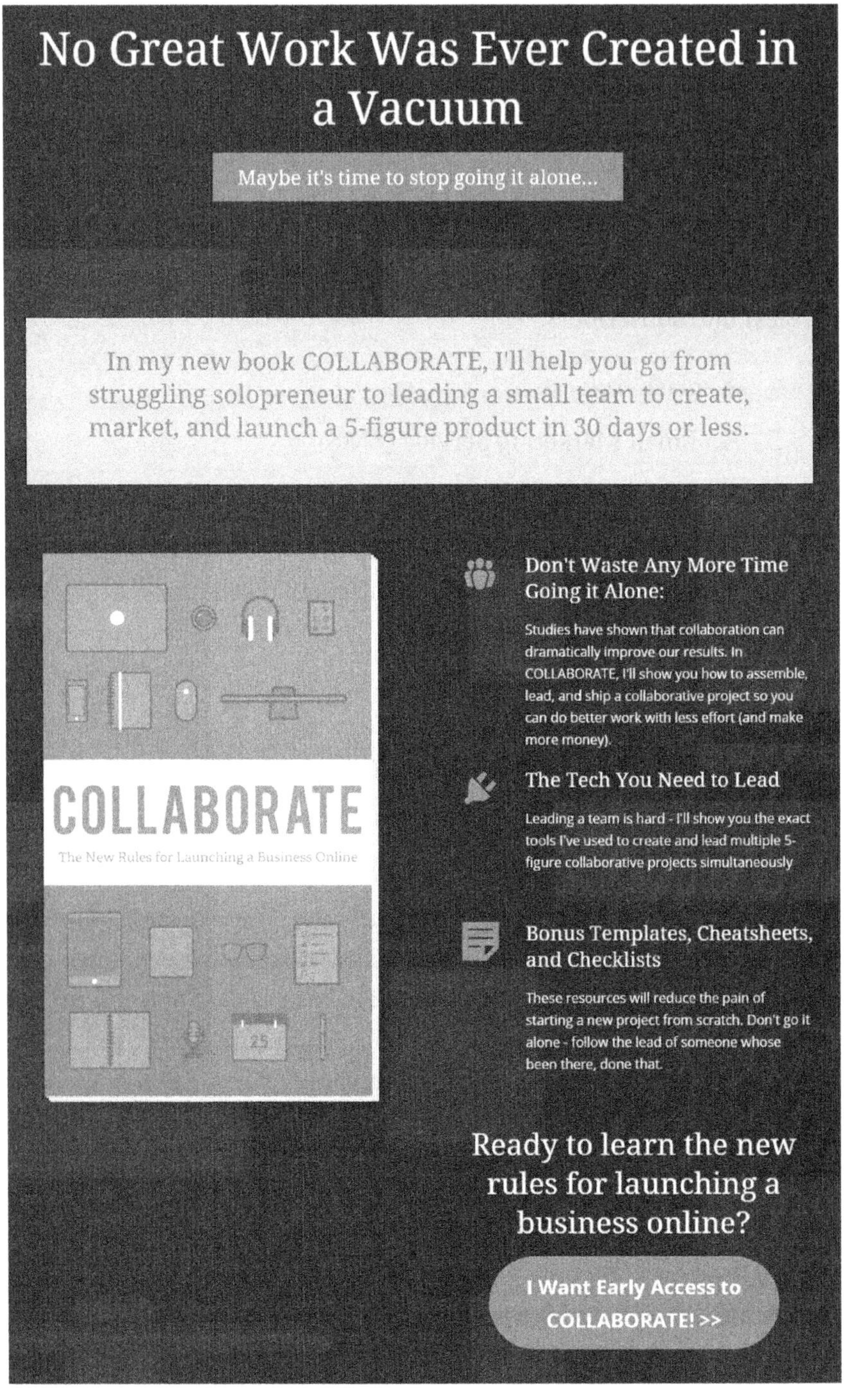
No Great Work Was Ever Created in a Vacuum
Maybe it's time to stop going it alone...
In my new book COLLABORATE, I'll help you go from struggling solopreneur to leading a small team to create, market, and launch a 5-figure product in 30 days or less.
COLLABORATE
The New Rules for Launching a Business Online
Don't Waste Any More Time Going it Alone:
Studies have shown that collaboration can dramatically improve our results. In COLLABORATE, I'll show you how to assemble, lead, and ship a collaborative project so you can do better work with less effort (and make more money).
The Tech You Need to Lead
Leading a team is hard - I'll show you the exact tools I've used to create and lead multiple 5-figure collaborative projects simultaneously
Bonus Templates, Cheatsheets, and Checklists
These resources will reduce the pain of starting a new project from scratch. Don't go it alone - follow the lead of someone whose been there, done that.
Ready to learn the new rules for launching a business online?
I Want Early Access to COLLABORATE! >>

I run all of my websites on WordPress because it's supported by thousands of developers, so I can always find someone to do whatever I need done. I recommend Wordpress if you're just starting out.

You can find WordPress at: www.WordPress.org

Leadpages

Leadpages is software that makes creating and deploying sales pages painless and fast. You can literally create a sales page in minutes, if not seconds, with Leadpages software. You don't even need to have a website to use Leadpages as they will host the pages for you (this is a very lean, very fast way to prototype and validate an idea). The downside is that it's an investment of about $30-$70 per month to get started.

Here's an example of a Leadpages page I was able to create in a few minutes:

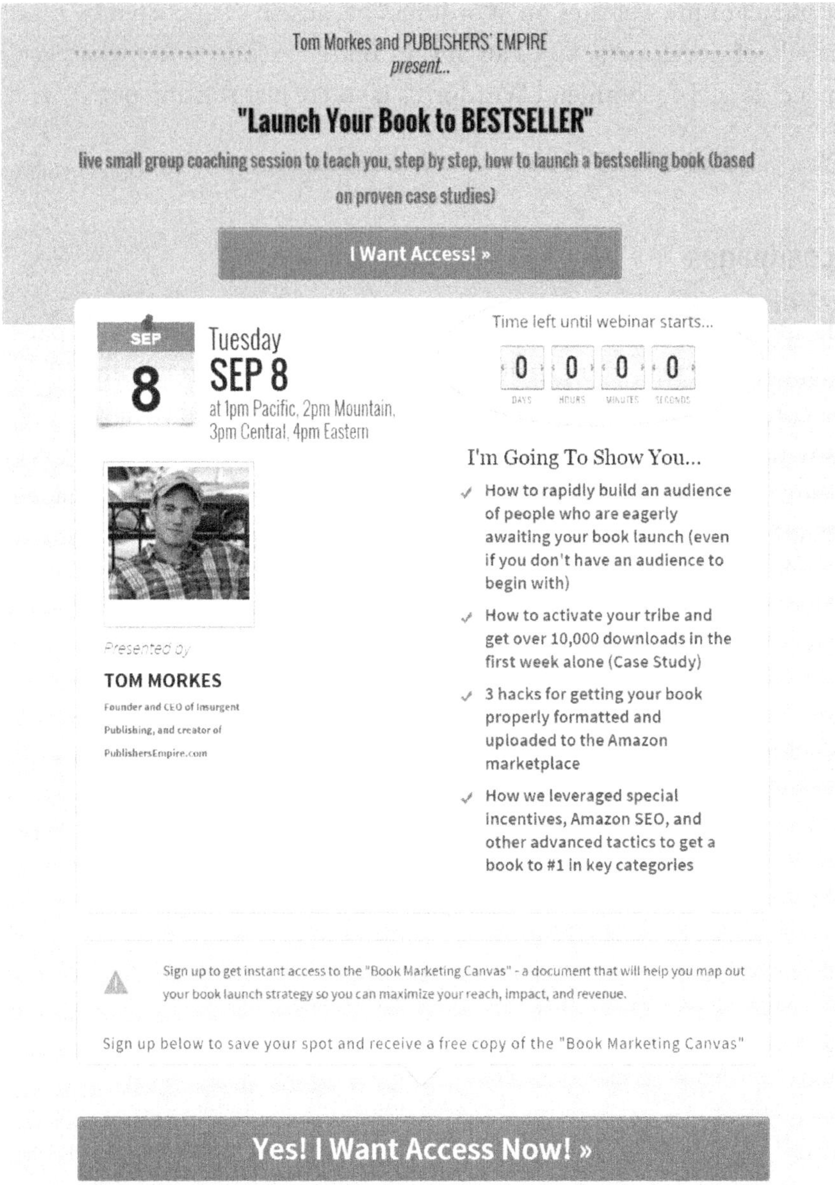
Tom Morkes and PUBLISHERS' EMPIRE
present...
"Launch Your Book to BESTSELLER"
live small group coaching session to teach you, step by step, how to launch a bestselling book (based on proven case studies)
I Want Access! »
SEP
8
Tuesday
SEP 8
at 1pm Pacific, 2pm Mountain, 3pm Central, 4pm Eastern
Time left until webinar starts...
0 0 0 0
DAYS HOURS MINUTES SECONDS
I'm Going To Show You...
How to rapidly build an audience of people who are eagerly awaiting your book launch (even if you don't have an audience to begin with)
How to activate your tribe and get over 10,000 downloads in the first week alone (Case Study)
3 hacks for getting your book properly formatted and uploaded to the Amazon marketplace
How we leveraged special incentives, Amazon SEO, and other advanced tactics to get a book to #1 in key categories
Presented by
TOM MORKES
Founder and CEO of Insurgent Publishing, and creator of PublishersEmpire.com
Sign up to get instant access to the "Book Marketing Canvas" - a document that will help you map out your book launch strategy so you can maximize your reach, impact, and revenue.
Sign up below to save your spot and receive a free copy of the "Book Marketing Canvas"
Yes! I Want Access Now! »

You can find Leadpages at: www.leadpages.net

Clickfunnels

Clickfunnels is similar to Leadpages but allows for more advanced customization. Clickfunnels not only allows you to build your entire funnel, from your Lead Capture Page, to your "thank you" page, to your webinar pages (if you're intending to use those to sell your product), but also comes with built in tracking that allows you to see where potential customers are leaving your site (allowing you to analyze the effectiveness of your entire sales funnel, whereas Leadpages can only track and measure individual pages). Like Leadpages, you don't need a website to host your pages; Clickfunnels can host them for you. Advanced features also include course and membership software. Pricing is steep, however, starting at $97per month starting (with the more advanced features requiring $297 per month).

You can find Clickfunnels at: www.clickfunnels.com

Email marketing service

Mailchimp

Mailchimp is a simple EMS that is free up to 2,000 subscribers, unless you want the ability to create autoresponder email sequences (then the price starts at $20 per month for 2,000 subscribers). I recommend Mailchimp if you're on a tight budget as they integrate with most mainstream software (including every splash page tool mentioned above).

You can find Mailchimp at: www.mailchimp.com

ConvertKit

ConvertKit is an email marketing service built for bloggers and authors. ConvertKit comes with great automation software allowing you to create robust email courses. This also comes with digital product delivery, unlike Mailchimp. There are also a near infinite number of ways to segment and filter your email list because of robust automation rules and a growing number of integrations. Finally, the ConvertKit UI is beautiful and easy to use, and the support team is responsive. Starting at $29 per month for up to 1,000 subscribers, ConvertKit is affordable even for bootstrapped projects.

You can find ConvertKit at: www.convertkit.com

Use the space below to outline the tools you will use to create your Lead Generation Page:

3. One Lead Conversion Process

The Lead Conversion Process refers to the way you will turn your subscribers into new buyers and happy customers.

Examples of Lead Conversion Processes include:

1. In person sales meeting

2. Sales call
3. Live webinar with sales pitch at the end
4. Email sequence with a sales pitch at the end
5. Video sales letter
6. Static sales page or sales letter

These are just a small sampling of the many ways to convert an interested person into a happy customer. Each are effective in their own way, but there is always a trade-off. For example, a static sales allows you to completely automate the sales process. Assuming you create a good sales page (i.e. one that converts visitors into buyers), this will lower your customer acquisition cost (the amount you need to pay to get one new paying customer), which will increase your overall profit margin (less overhead and expenses equals more profit for everyone). However, because most sales pages convert at a lower rate than alternative Lead Conversion Processes, you may not generate enough sales to make your launch profitable.

The following chart is a reference point to help you get started:

Type	Difficulty	Effectiveness	Scalability	Ideal price
Static sales page	Low	Low	High	Low
Automated email sequence	Moderate	Moderate	High	Low / Moderate
Video training series	High	Moderate	High	Low / Moderate
Live webinar	Moderate	High	Moderate	Moderate
Phone	Moderate	Very High	Low	High
In person	Moderate	Very High	Very Low	Very High

Lead Conversion Process

One of my clients had a relatively large, engaged audience (about 10,000 subscribers). He wanted to launch a new product, so he created a sales page, and emailed his email list about the new product (using all the techniques outlined previously to generate interest, increase perceived value, urgency, scarcity, etc.). After emailing his list multiple times, he converted at about 1% of his total list.

1% of 10,000 people = 100 sales.

Decent, but not great (not for that sized email list, at least).

After analyzing the funnel, we decided to implement a more manual, high-touch Lead Conversion Process. We decided to use a live webinar with a sales pitch at the end. The result?

Sales went from 1% to 2.5%. This was a 250% increase in sales, and 150 new customers he wouldn't have had otherwise. Did the webinar take longer? Yes, but for my client, this was a small price to pay to more than double his customer base right from the start.

The key here isn't to get hung up on which Lead Conversion Process is best, but to choose one and then test and measure it, making tweaks and adjustments as you go.

Use the space below to outline your Lead Conversion Process:

Why the 1-1-1 Product Launch Method works

The 1-1-1 Product Launch Method works for two primary reasons:

First, by focusing on just a few key items, you can better execute and measure what you are doing. Being able to properly execute and measure your results will lead to better learning. Over the long haul, learning inevitably leads to success.

Second, the process is manageable. Most solopreneur launches fail because of user-error. In other words, the launch is overcomplicated with too many variables, requiring too much time and effort to track, implement, and manage. The launch fails because the individual is overwhelmed and can't properly execute nor measure his results. By focusing on just a single funnel with just three elements, you and your team of collaborators can execute with precision.

Remember, for a collaboration, speed is key. That's why it's essential you focus your time, money, and effort on the simplest, most direct route to your goal. The 1-1-1 Product Launch Method will help you get there.

Azimuth Check

When you begin selling, think about how you can use proven psychological triggers to encourage your customers to buy now, not later. Follow the 1-1-1 Product Launch Method in order to streamline your product launch. There are a lot of options available to anyone launching a product online—don't overcomplicate things. Choose the tools you will use and stick to them. Focus your efforts on the 20% of actions that will produce 80% of your results. When in doubt, make sure you're focusing on the best possible customer experience.

Take a short break to take notes and add your thoughts below before moving onto the next Milestone:

Milestone purpose

To show you how to sell your product to increase your chances of success.

Milestone checklist

- [ ] Conduct a dry run rehearsal
- [ ] Feed the funnel
- [ ] Close the sale

MILESTONE 12

PRE-SELL YOUR PRODUCT

Let's take a quick pause to reflect on your journey up to this Milestone.

By this point, you've done the following:

1. Conducted self-analysis to determine your personal and business goals
2. Brainstormed and developed a profitable idea
3. Defined your ideal collaborator and reached out to build a relationship with him or her
4. Collaboratively developed your idea into a one page business plan
5. Defined your Minimum Viable Product (MVP)
6. Turned your MVP into a product wireframe and sales and marketing wireframe

7. Turned your wireframes into Key Objectives, Tasks Lists, a Project Timeline, and a Project Management Board
8. Developed your Standard Operating Procedures
9. Used the 1-1-1 Product Launch Method to begin turning your plans into a practical sales funnel

You really ought to take a moment to congratulate yourself; very few people will make it this far in the collaborative product launch process. Most people have fizzled out by now, but not you. You should be proud.

But, you still have work to do...

You've come a long way, and now it's time to launch your product and close your first sale (or better yet, first 100).

Before you open up your launch sequence, you're going to want to do a couple things.

Conduct a dry run rehearsal

A dry run is a term commonly used in the U.S. Army to refer to the practice round before a mission, event, or training exercise. For example, when running a live-fire marksmanship range (i.e. shooting at plastic, green pop-up targets), it's standard practice for those running the event to walk through how the training event will unfold, from setup to shut down, so that both the training facilitators and the training participants know what to expect. This cuts down on the potential for errors, and increases the potential for a successful operation.

While it's not life and death with online business, you should take the time to run through your launch with your collaborators before you open it up to real people. This will help you find and fix any potential problems with your sales funnel.

Note: there are always problems with every project, so don't skip this step!

How to conduct a dry run rehearsal

Step 1. Review all systems and software

Spend one to two hours making sure your systems and software are set up correctly. This could be as simple as making sure the backend for the software you're working with is properly registered, that you have the right integrations in place, and that everything appears to be working.

Step 2. Walk through the process as a customer

Next, have you and your collaborators each individually go through the funnel as if they were customers. If you're running Facebook ads, for example, make sure the ad is live, then share the live link with your collaborators to click through and walk through the process; signup through every optin box; make sure all pages and links are working; double check that everything is working on the backend (i.e. is your email optin collecting and saving emails properly?), etc. The goal here is to both see how it feels from the customer's point of view to enter your sales funnel, as well as make sure there are no user-facing errors in your funnel.

Questions you want to answer:

Focus	Questions	Answer
Dry run rehearsal	Are all links working?	
	Are all graphics in place?	
	Is there a clear Call to Action at every point in the process?	
	Is it clear what is happening? Are the next steps clear?	

Step 3. Wargame possible scenarios

Spend one hour with your collaborators to come up with possible scenarios where your launch could fail. Once you have these written down, write down ways you can (1) mitigate this from ever happening, and (2) find a backup solution to keep everything working.

Questions you should consider:

Focus	Questions	Answer
Wargaming possible scenarios	What if the server gets overloaded and shuts down?	
	What happens if the ecommerce solution stops working?	
	What happens if the webinar ends half-way through, or the auto-responder doesn't send, or a link ends up broken?	
	What don't we know for sure right now? Do we need to consider any of these items?	

Use the following space to make additional notes or brainstorm other possible errors and corresponding solutions:

Step 4. Troubleshoot and fix any existing problems

Finally, fix all errors that you've found. In regards to the potential problems that might occur, develop at least one fallback solution that everyone in the group is comfortable with. Make sure all collaborators understand the funnel process, and what to do in case something breaks or stops working.

Dry run rehearsal checklist

The following is a generic checklist for you to use for your project. You should use this as a starting point, but then modify and adopt for your own use.

Dry run rehearsal checklist		
Focus	**Questions**	**Answer**
Lead generator	Are the components of our Lead Generator built?	
	If doing paid advertising, are the ads setup properly and cleared to work? e.g. if using Facebook Ads, have they been cleared by Facebook?	
	Is the Call to Action for the Lead Generator clear and compelling?	
	Are all images formatted properly?	
	Are all links working?	

Lead capture	Does the url for our Lead Capture Page open?	
	Does the page load quickly?	
	Does the optin form work properly? Does it link to a thank you page?	
	Does the optin form collect email addresses properly? Does it integrate with your email marketing service?	
	Is there a clear call to action on the Lead Capture Page (sign up now)? On the thank you page (share)?	
	Is there a follow up email that goes out to subscribers to confirm they are on the right list? Does it include another clear Call to Action (share, download bonus, etc.)?	
Lead conversion	Is the pitch created and ready?	
	Are all presentation materials created and properly formatted?	
	Is the Call to Action clear?	
	Does the ecommerce solution work? Can you make a purchase now?	
	What happens after someone purchases? Are they taken to a thank you page?	
	Does the product deliver immediately? Or is there an immediate follow up to congratulate your new customer on making the right choice?	
	Can you track this process so you can personally reach out to early adopters and thank them?	

Once you've finished your final Dry Run Rehearsal and fixed any errors or issues, it's time to start the launch...

Feed the funnel

At this point, everything should be set up and ready to go; you've now set up all the key elements of your launch, you've walked through the process as a customer, and there is nothing left to troubleshoot.

Now it's time to push the play button and follow through with your launch.

This means you need to initiate your Lead Generator to start collecting email addresses. From here, you should move the subscribers into your Lead Conversion Process, whether live webinar, static sales page, sales call, or something else. Because of how you've built everything up to this point, this process should be essentially automatic; the real work has already been done. Now you just need to make sure people are moving through your funnel and to the Lead Conversion Process (closing the sale).

Close the sale

Selling is as much art as it is science. That's why it's best to focus on practical strategies that have been proven to close sales time and time again. While your particular Lead Conversion technique may vary (sales page versus webinar versus phone call, etc.), the elements in closing a sale are the same.

Step 1. Listen

The key here is listen to the potential customer's problem. Your goal is to get the person to deep-dive into their problems so you can get a very good understanding of the issues they're facing and what's holding them back (so you know if you can help them or not).

If you've done your research and iteratively validated your profitable idea as you built it, your sales page, webinar, or pitch should pinpoint the customer's pain as if you've known them your entire life.

Step 2. Relate

The key here is to be human. It sounds silly to say out loud, but the reality is so many people doing business online immediately turn to sounding like a corporate robot. This is a mistake. Once you understand the customer's problem, you need to be able to show them that you understand how they feel.

Whether you're closing the sale over the phone or on a webpage, the key is to respond to your customer using the same words and style they use. You not only want to show them you understand what their problem is, but that you understand them at a subconscious level. In person, this is where using the same body language helps dramatically. For digital sales, it means using the same words and grammar that your customer uses.

Step 3. Transition

Once you understand the customer's problem, you know where they want to be, and you're confident your product or service can get them there, now it's time to transition to the sale. This means explaining to them how your particular product or service will get them the results they want and avoid the pitfalls of prior solutions.

What if nobody buys?

First, I doubt this will happen. If you have iteratively tested your product as you created it (i.e. creating the simplest Minimum Viable

Product, getting feedback from real customers right from the start, etc.), then chances are somebody will buy (because someone should have already bought).

But if for some reason you sell less than expected, you may need to Pivot.

Pivot 101

Eric Ries is a tech startup founder, the bestselling author of *The Lean Startup*, and a thought leader in the Lean Startup movement. Ries defines a Pivot as a "structured course correction designed to test a new fundamental hypothesis about the product, strategy, and engine of growth."[1]

In other words, a Pivot is adjusting your current approach to a problem. In this case, it means adjusting the Lead Generator to Lead Capture process.

How to make a Pivot

Step 1. Identify what is not working.

Did your Lead Generator fail to deliver enough subscribers? Did your optin bribe on your Lead Capture Page fail to get people to subscribe? Or did your Lead Conversion Process simply fail to get someone to invest their time and money into your product?

The beauty of the 1-1-1 Product Launch Method is that by focusing on one Lead Generator, one Lead Capture Page, and one Lead Conversion Process you can find out relatively quickly what is working and what is not. For example, if you find that people aren't signing up, it must be either a problem with your Lead Generator or the Lead Capture Page. From here, you can hone in on each element individually to see if there are any technical issues, or if it's a marketing issue.

The 80/20 principle applies to failure too. Chances are there are one or two things keeping your project from succeeding, which is why you want to fix those one or two things and ignore everything else.

Step 2. Relaunch your product as soon as possible.

A relaunch could be as simple as a new series of emails, a new live webinar, or a new promotional effort (with a new marketing angle). The key here is to figure out what must be fixed and then get it out to your ideal customer as fast as possible.

Pivoting High Speed Elite

With High Speed Elite, our first live webinar was basically a flop; we had only one student enroll and pay for the program. If you recall, our minimum criterion to move forward with the program was five student pre-orders. With a webinar of 30 people, surely we should have closed more sales. That's when we Pivoted on our message; we had originally focused on all military veterans who were currently transitioning from active duty to civilian. That was a broad, nebulous segment of the military population. Our live webinar was too generic, too broad.

After the results of our first webinar, we immediately shifted focus to where our greatest strength and focused lied: business and entrepreneurship. We updated our slides, changed our Facebook advertising to focus on entrepreneurship, and adjusted some of our sales copy to better reflect the new business angle. Our next webinar brought in six more sales, for a total of seven students for our first class. We couldn't have done it without Pivoting.

Questions to consider before Pivoting:

Spend 30-60 minutes with your collaborators to discuss the following questions and define a series of follow on steps to implement changes in your process.

Focus	Questions	Answer
Pivot questions	What are the results of our current Lead Generation efforts?	
	Where are we losing customers? Are they dropping off once they get to our Lead Capture Page? Or are they not even clicking through our Lead Generator?	
	What can we change right now that could positively affect click through? What about conversion?	
	Can we test out another Lead Generator quickly and cheaply to see if that makes a difference?	

Whatever you discover from this collaborative brainstorming session, do what you can to implement changes immediately. To do this, prioritize changes based on what you believe could make the biggest impact and which are the easiest to implement. Referring back to the 80/20 principle, it's better to fix only 20% of things that could improve conversion by 80% than try to work on the 80% of small factors that lead to only 20% of the results.

Pivoting after launch

Remember Kira from Polymer Clay TV? Kira and her business partner, Lisa, had been producing their Youtube video each week for years. However, they gave these videos away for free and found their Etsy shop wasn't making them the money they needed to continue. They needed to Pivot.

That's when Kira developed the idea to create a unique experience for artists everywhere to learn from each other. Lisa and Kira reached out to great artists from around the world and asked them to create tutorial videos for people to watch and learn from at home. Once they had a team of people ready to join in, they created the Polymer Clay Adventure, a video workshop series for artists. This Pivot allowed them to turn their YouTube followers into paying customers, and a $50,000 launch.

Final thoughts on Pivoting

Don't be afraid to Pivot and don't be too proud to change what you're doing. It's important to note that, more likely than not, some part of your original configuration is working. In order to make the right changes quickly, focus on making small changes before making big changes (i.e. changing the text of the sales copy before redesigning the entire sales page). Never be afraid to change directions if there current path is not getting you where you need to go.

Azimuth Check

Before you launch your product, complete a Dry Run Rehearsal with your collaborators to ensure everything is working property. When everyone has had a chance to walk through the sales funnel as a customer, decide what needs to be changed or fixed (if anything). Then it's time to pull the trigger. Pay attention to the process and actions you are taking; measure the results. See how your launch goes and take note if you need to make a Pivot. Listen to what your customers are saying and, most importantly, what they are doing. If you are not seeing the sales you want, relaunch as quickly as possible.

Take a short break here to take notes or add your thoughts below before moving onto the next Milestone:

PHASE 5

ACCELERATE

Milestone 13: Onboard New Customers

Milestone 14: Review, Evaluate, Improve, Grow

Milestone purpose

To show you how to delight your customers and deliver on your promises.

Milestone checklist

- [ ] Conduct new user onboarding
- [ ] Crowdsource product development
- [ ] Iteratively deliver your product

MILESTONE 13

ONBOARD NEW CUSTOMERS

"Onboarding, also known as organizational socialization, refers to the mechanism through which new employees acquire the necessary knowledge, skills, and behaviors to become effective organizational members and insiders." —Wikipedia.org[1]

Onboarding traditionally applies to integrating new employees into the corporate climate, but the term has recently evolved to apply to new customers of software products, especially Software as a Service (SaaS) applications. I want to take it one step further and apply user onboarding to early adopters who pre-order a product or service based on a promise from a company or individual.

Conduct new user onboarding

You've built your MVP, which is nothing more than a shell of the actual product, and you've asked your early adopters to invest in it in exchange for something extra (early access, a special discounted price, or even the simple pride of knowing they're a founding member). It is especially important to make sure these early adopters are satisfied with their purpose. That's why user onboarding is even more crucial in this scenario—your trust is on the line. You've promised something and you have to deliver. If you don't, you are essentially breaking a promise. If that happens, you may permanently damage the relationship with your early adopters, people you need to be successful.

You can avoid the most dangerous pitfalls of user onboarding by abiding by the following three principles:

1. Over-engage
2. Over-personalize
3. Over-deliver

We'll break them down one at a time:

Step 1. Over-engage

There is no such thing as too much communication, especially when delivering a Minimum Viable Product to a new set of customers. For example, don't be afraid to send email updates several times a week. Eventually, you can automate this process as you refine your systems and onboarding process. For now, high-touch, manual outreach is okay. The goal is to make sure all your customers know what's going on. You want it to be impossible for your customers to *not* know how much work you're putting into the project and into their success.

Use the space below to outline your plan to over-engage with your early adopters:

How we over-engaged with new students in High Speed Elite

For High Speed Elite, we were able to over-engage with early adopters during the onboarding process by reaching out to them several times a week to give them updates on the progress of the business course we were building, to share progress on the platform we were building, and any new initiatives we were undertaking to help them take their results to the next level. It seems simple, but an individualized email once or twice a week can work wonders for your customers and early adopters.

Step 2. Over-personalize

Your major advantage as a small, collaborative team is that you can do the things that big business can't. And guess what? Early adopters love this.

Here are some ways to over-personalize through your onboarding process:

1. Send a personal email
2. Send a personal text message
3. Use the person's name in live training
4. Let this person engage back
5. Reach out for personal feedback and put the feedback into practice (How am I doing? What can I do better?)
6. Send a personal thank you note.

The opportunities to over-personalize are endless. Make sure you take advantage of this as this is one area in particular no big business can beat you. Take the time you need to give direct attention to your early adopters and they will reward you with the best help you can get: word-of-mouth referrals.

Use the space below to outline your plan to over-personalize the onboarding process:

High Speed Elite and over-personalizing our message

For High Speed Elite, the emails we sent to early adopters were all individualized. We also connected via Facebook, phone, Skype, etc. for one-on-one calls. We frequently asked for feedback and then acted on that feedback to make the program better. The entire experience was as personalized as we could make it.

Step 3. Over-deliver

"You should take extraordinary measures not just to acquire users, but also to make them happy."—Paul Graham, Y Combinator

Bottom line: you should do everything in your power to make sure anyone who supported you before you had a tested, proven product, gets the best service. They deserve at least this for trusting you enough with their time and money on something that might not work.

Some ways to over-deliver:

1. Grandfather in early, discounted rates (for memberships or software)
2. Provide one-on-one attention and/or direct access to you
3. Give them bonuses (additional materials, features, or products for which you would normally charge extra)

These are just a few of the ways you can over-deliver. If you're not sure how to over-deliver, ask your early adopters what they need or want to help them get better results from your product or service. This will give you a good indication of what you can do to over-deliver for them.

Use the space below to outline your plan to over-deliver for your early adopters:

Over-delivering for High Speed Elite students

For High Speed Elite, we focused on giving our early adopters as much personalized, one-on-one attention as we could. The purpose of our program was to help veterans build businesses. Because we were offering small group coaching and helping people build businesses, this additional one-on-one attention added significant value.

While providing extra one-on-one attention wasn't easy (it is not scalable and can take a lot of time when you do this for months with multiple students), it resulted in powerful, compelling testimonials. This in turn made launching v2.0 of High Speed Elite much easier because we had great word-of-mouth referrals behind our work.

How Popcorn Metrics used user onboarding to increase conversions over 300%

Paul Boyce is the founder and CEO of Popcorn Metrics, a software company that makes integrating advanced web analytics into your website fast and easy, without any code.

When Boyce first opened up Popcorn Metrics, many of his initial beta testers became their biggest fans. However, as time went on they were finding it difficult to convert users from a free trial to a paid account. After weeks of focusing on this problem to figure out ways to increase retention (people staying with the platform beyond the free trial), Boyce finally spotted the problem. While his service is relatively low cost (about $50 per month), it required a level of high-touch engagement to properly onboard new users. The software itself wasn't complex, but what it could do could make it seem complex. Boyce had spent a lot of direct time with his beta users showing them how to make everything work—that's why they stuck around. New users weren't getting the same experience. By shifting to high-touch user onboarding (see: over-engaging, over-personalizing, and over-delivering), Boyce was able to increase conversion by 300%.

Here's Boyce's biggest takeaway from his dramatic increase in sales and retention:

"Build your customer onboarding process with the single goal of helping users become successful in their job, help make it easy for them, and if you can do that—then they'll become your customer as a natural consequence. Even better, you'll have customers that you've invested time in and started building a trusting relationship that should last a long time—as both yours and their business grows."

When asked to elaborate on the most important aspects of user onboarding to increase sales and retention, Boyce elaborate:

"Three things:

1. Easy to schedule or ideally real-time; we use a combination of Live Chat (livechatinc.com) for in the moment [engagement] and YouCanBook.me for scheduling deeper sessions [with customers] at a convenient time.
2. Easy to connect with people (i.e. low-friction). That means pick up the phone, or use something like appear.in for instant, low-friction, face-to-face conversation, easy screen share (for demos/problem resolving), etc.
3. All about the user. We don't really give generic demos. It's more like:

   'ok, where are you now?'

   'what are you trying to achieve?'

   'ok, here's how I can help you with that...'

   And then be very specific to that customer."

Crowdsource product development

At this point, you've launched your product and you have paying customers, but the core of the product still needs to be built. The next step is to use your early customers as a sounding board for the product you're creating for them. You can do this through crowdsourcing your product development.

What is crowdsourcing?

"the practice of obtaining needed services, ideas, or content by soliciting contributions from a large group of people and especially from the online community rather than from traditional employees or suppliers." —Merriam-Webster[2]

In other words, crowdsourcing lets us build something cost-effectively by leveraging the strengths of many people who help on a voluntary basis. More important than the cost savings, crowdsourcing can allow you to develop a much better product because your customers are the ones who provide the direct insight into what they want, because they are helping you create it.

Why crowdsource your product?

Crowdsourcing is very powerful, but must be managed properly. To clarify, the point of crowdsourcing is not to shift all the work to your customers. Do that and you'll get burned (and rightly so). The purpose behind crowdsourcing your product development is threefold:

#1. Create a more focused, better product for your users

No more need to guess what you should be building; simply asking will give you a plethora of responses.

#2. Create faster through customer involvement

If you crowdsource correctly, leveraging the high-touch onboarding process mentioned in the previous section, you won't have to wait around for weeks to figure out what to tackle next. Instead, direct access to your customers will help you deploy something and get instantaneous feedback.

#3. Build lifetime customers and massively loyal fans

Early adopters love to be a part of product development. Many entrepreneurs fail to realize this and instead build in a bubble. This is a bad idea because not only do your early adopters want to know what you're doing (and often—how you're doing it), most of them would appreciate being involved in the decision making of how the product is built. This is not to say you should build whatever your early adopters tell you to build. Rather, many of your early adopters will enjoy giving input and will feel great if you simply listen to them and take their input into consideration as you build the product or service.

How to Crowdsource your product development

Here are just a few ways you can crowdsource product development:

1. Ask for feedback on your design
2. Hold a competition to see who can come up with the best name or description or tagline for your product
3. Hold a competition for the logo or product design
4. Ask for feedback on your sales page
5. Ask for a video testimonial on why your users signed up for your product or service, and why they would recommend it to others
6. Ask for user input on what they think is the best way to market and sell your product (this can lead to some really great ideas)
7. Ask people to share resources that helped them with X (whatever it is you're solving)
8. Share a working document with people and ask them to review, give feedback, comment, or edit as they like
9. Let your users help edit and write your book, or code your product (if you're building something open-source), etc.

There are hundreds of ways to crowdsource the development of your product.

Use the following space to brainstorm ways you can crowdsource the development of your product:

Crowdsourcing the development of Webinar Ninja

Omar Zenhom, CEO and founder of Webinar Ninja, on how he crowdsourced the development of his flagship software:

"About a year ago, we launched a webinar platform called Webinar Ninja. It was a very, very small launch; we did a beta test and we only opened it up for 100 users. The purpose of this whole thing was to see how much people would pay, and to see if we could handle this business in terms of customer service, emails, support, upgrades, and maintaining our staff when it comes to programmers. You have to find out if you can pull [a business]off, or actually make money from it.

Once we discovered some of the things that we didn't like about our [Minimum Viable Product] thanks to feedback from that small group about what they think of the software and improvements, we had to iterate. The whole point in this situation is that I'm keeping it small because if there is any damage, if there's anything going on, if, for example, I decide, after I launch it, I don't want to do this anymore, I'm not enjoying this, or this is not what it's turning out to be, you can just say to them: 'You know, listen, we'll support you with the software for the next year, but we're going to back off of it because we decided to shift directions.'

That's a lot easier when you have 100 users versus 1,000, or 10,000 users.

On the other side of it, we learned a lot of positive things and said 'Okay, great, now we know which direction to go. We know what's important to our users. We know exactly how to do it.'

So we did another small launch group, opened it up for another 100 users, and then we launched version 1.0. After that, we polished version 2.0; made some improvements, fixed some bugs, and made sure everything was working properly.

For example, we had some prominent players that use webinars, so we had them test it out on a more high-stakes platform to see if it's stable. Now we're working on a major overhaul of this product, version 3.0, which is what I had always wanted to build, but I couldn't start there, because I didn't know yet what this thing actually was just yet. I had to hear from my audience, I had to figure it out step by step."

Zenhom elaborates on why he started with a Minimum Viable Product and how he used crowdsourcing to iteratively build the final product:

"I'd rather start with something minimal. When I came out with the first version, the beta version, there were a lot of features that were not there. I was upset. It was like, 'these features are important, I should have these features, right?'

But I had to make the decision: 'No, the bare minimum stuff, make sure that it works properly.'

Sometimes we think that customers will go crazy if we don't have all the features: 'I can't believe this doesn't do this! I can't believe this doesn't have this!'

Right? It turns out, it's okay, people are going to be fine.

Why?

Because you can iterate.

You can add the additional features later; you can launch a new feature in the next update. The point is you need to work your way to the final product, making baby steps. This will help you not make as many mistakes along the way, and allow you to clean up quickly if you make a mistake; you can improve and pivot if you need to.

The best example I can give is, if you remember when you were a kid, you were learning long division in school.

The teacher would tell you, step by step, how to do long division. Carry the one, and then how many times does five go into twenty-five, things like that, right? So, if you got the wrong answer, the teacher would tell you, 'Okay, let's look back at your work.'

That's why they say, 'Show your work.'

It allows us to see what mistakes we made along the way; 'In step five, you made a mistake here.'

So the point is that, if you don't go step-by-step and show your work, you're not going to be able to see where you went wrong, and where your business failed. You can't remedy big mistakes if you just go from nothing to version 5.0. You can't just solve the equation with no work involved, because if it fails, you're going to think, 'Oh this failed, I gotta move on.'

But really, you have no idea what happened."

Iteratively deliver your product

As Omar Zenhom, CEO and founder of Webinar Ninja, stated in the previous section, focusing on the final version of your product ("version 5.0") instead of the first iteration, your Minimum Viable Product (or "version 1.0") is a mistake. You will never be able to build your dream solution (product or service) in your first go. If you do, you have wasted time, money, and effort, because if you're building the final version, you don't have time to actually test and measure what you're building with current users.

User onboarding not only helps with creating better products with less waste while building a massively loyal fan base, it also lets you ship smaller, progressively improved versions of your product as you build them. This is what we call iterative product development and delivery.

What is iteration?

"The action or a process of iterating or repeating a procedure in which repetition of a sequence of operations yields results successively closer to a desired result."—Merriam-Webster[3]

For your collaborative product, iteration is about defining your perfect product, reducing it to its core (the Minimum Viable Product), and then progressively improving the product in stages until you reach your perfect product (or, what is more likely the case, figuring out a better direction for your product because of the rapid learning you are exposed to while iterating your product).

Why iterate?

"We tend to think of seminal innovation...such as the release of the Apple II personal computer in 1977, as proverbial lightbulb moments. Yet the truth behind a device like the Apple II isn't Steve Jobs and Steve Wozniak as transcendent inventors, but a culmination of 30 years of iterative product development and failure in the highly complementary transistor industry—for example, the pair's influential visit to Douglas Engelbart's lab at Stanford Research Institute where they first glimpsed a Graphical User Interface (GUI) and the mouse."[4]

Contrary to popular belief, impressive improvements in any industry are less a result of genius innovation and more a result of calculated, iterative development.

Iteration allows you to focus your effort on incremental progress; instead of needing to have everything perfect, you can create the 20% of things that create 80% of value for your customers. By focusing on incremental progress, you can work faster and more inexpensively, while learning at a more rapid rate than traditional product development processes allow.

In the context of collaboration, iteration will allow you to move faster, produce better, and enjoy the process because you're consistently improving the life of your customer through your progressive improvements.

How to iterate

Successful iteration requires you to focus on user success, first and foremost, in conjunction with the 80/20 principle. The question you should ask is: "what do my users need and want the most, and what is the simplest improvement we can make that will produce the most progress for them right now?"

Iteration is usually done through one or more of the following:

1. Developing a new feature
2. Fixing a bug
3. Improving the user interface
4. Improving documentation
5. Refining or streamlining a system or process

Once you've defined what it is you want to add, remove, or improve, it's time to decide which particular changes will create the greatest amount of additional value to your customer.

Here's how to plan your iteration process:

1. Create a list of potential improvements for your current product
2. Define the value-addition of each improvement, and rank them from 1 to 10 (1 being the smallest value increase to the customer, 10 being the greatest value increase to the customer)
3. Define the resource-intensiveness of each improvement, and rank them based on how much time, money, and effort each improvement will take (1 being less time, money, and effort, 10 being the most time, money, and effort)
4. Collaboratively discuss and decide on priorities of work (i.e. which improvement will you focus solely on for the next iteration)
5. Write down the due date for the completion and release of the next product iteration

Use the space below to plan your iteration process:

Supercharging your iteration

Continuously improving and releasing new versions of your product is a great way to make early adopters feel like they have gotten their money's worth from their initial investment. However, it's also an amazing opportunity to relaunch your more complete solution to a new group of potential customers.

Use major product improvements to relaunch your product to new potential customers using the exact same process you did for your original launch.

Use the space below to define new potential product Milestones that may lend themselves to a relaunch of your product:

Azimuth Check

Fundamentally, the purpose of user onboarding is to create the most value possible for your current customers. By over-engaging, over-personalizing, and over-delivering, you create a remarkable experience that will endear you and your team to your customers. By crowd-sourcing product development, not only will you create your product faster and better (immediate user feedback creates the chance for rapid learning, improvement, and thus iteration), but you also make your customers part of the product itself, making them more committed to its success. This can lead to powerful word-of-mouth marketing. After your MVP has launched, use iterative product development to continue to build and release a new, better product for your customers. If you can, take advantage of major iteration Milestones to relaunch your product again.

Take a short break here to take notes or add your thoughts below before moving onto the next Milestone:

Milestone purpose

To help you productively review your collaboration to drive future success.

Milestone checklist

- [ ] Conduct your After Action Review
- [ ] Calculate project Return on Investment
- [ ] Determine next steps for your collaboration

MILESTONE 14

REVIEW, EVALUATE, IMPROVE, GROW

Congratulations, you've made it to the final Milestone. That means you've launched and have generated real learning from real customers, and, ideally, earned a healthy amount of profit for your efforts. Whether or not that last part is true, you've come to the point where you need to decide "what happens to this project now?"

Fundamentally, this Milestone is about analyzing, evaluating, and deciding on one of the following courses of action:

1. Do you continue with the next version of your collaborative product with the same team?
2. Do you continue with the next version of your product or service but independently of your collaborative group?
3. Do you scrap the project and move onto something else?

To clarify: there is no wrong answer here.

Even if you generated over $100,000 from your collaborative launch, you may have found the process less than ideal for your situation; perhaps one of your team members ended up being a bad fit; perhaps the effort you put in was not worth the reward.

While I have tried my best to mitigate these potential pitfalls for you in this guide book, nothing is guaranteed. Such is life and entrepreneurship.

Now is the time to take stock of where you are and where you want to go, in business and life.

Let's get to it...

Conduct your After Action Review

An After Action Review (AAR) is a retrospective analysis framework used by modern militaries to evaluate the success or failure of a training exercise or combat mission. While the AAR was developed by military commanders for wartime analysis, it is not uncommon to see the framework used by corporations and businesses to improve operational effectiveness and leadership within an organization. The reason for this is simple: the framework is easy to apply yet highly effective at objectively evaluating a given operation (in this case, your collaborative product launch).

The AAR Format

The AAR is broken down into four primary questions that must be addressed by all relevant parties (i.e. anyone who participated in your project in a key role). They are the following:

Question 1. What was supposed to happen?

In order for an AAR to be effective, there must be a benchmark or standard by which to measure performance. Earlier in this book, you learned how to set measurable goals and to define your desired end-state. This is precisely what you would want to state or write down as you begin the AAR process.

Question 2. What did happen?

At this point, an objective review of your collaborative project should take place.

What happened as you assembled your group? What happened as you planned your project? What happened when you created your MVP? What happened as you built your sales funnel and tested it? What happened when you finally launched?

Make sure to explain in detail or write down specifically what occurred, with as much qualified data (e.g. conversion rates, sales rates, revenue, expenses) as possible.

Question 3. What went well? What should we sustain for future projects?

Every key player present during this AAR should list off at least three "Sustains" for the project, or three things that the team did really well. Focus on major areas of planning and execution where your team effort directly created a desired result. For example, if you generated a lot of highly-targeted traffic through your sales funnel, a sustain would be "traffic strategy and execution."

The best analysis will focus on specific processes that worked well (achieved or surpassed your original goals), as well as specific actions taken by individual collaborators. Feel free to champion individuals in this question.

Question 4. What didn't work? What can we improve for future projects?

Every key player present during this AAR should list off at three "Improves" for the project. An "Improve" is any area or activity, process, or action that did not achieve its goal or reach your predefined standard. For example, if you were unable to sell a single product, an Improve would be "closing the sale."

As above, focus on major areas of planning and execution. The best analysis will focus on specific processes that did not go according to plan. While it is useful to focus on people and processes when discussing Sustains, it is better to focus entirely on processes for recommended improvements. AARs that focus on individual participants quickly degrade into an argument, reducing the effectiveness of the AAR and creating bitterness or anger between collaborators. The goal of the person leading the AAR should be to keep everything professional by focusing on specific, constructive critiques of processes and systems as a whole.

A quick note on "Improves"

The purpose of the AAR is to learn, not to place blame. That means even if your project failed (or didn't do as well as you and your collaborators had hoped), it is still a chance to learn. Matt Helbig, founder of Valid 8, believes that failures are great learning experiences. "The best way I think for most people to learn is actually going through, and failing, and trying, and thrashing, and struggling and doing all that, because you learn on the way. Then, maybe one day, when you do have a better idea, you're better positioned to execute in the future."

Who should be present?

All key players of a project should be present for an AAR. For a collaborative business project, that would be everyone directly involved in the project (the original founders or partners), as well as any essential contractors or outside partners if they had a big part in the launch of your project.

Who should lead the AAR?

In most cases, anyone involved in the collaborative project could facilitate and lead an AAR. However, for the sake of consistency, it is generally best to let the lead operator (usually the project manager of the collaborative project) lead the discussion. While this person will lead the discussion, all parties involved are responsible for contributing to the successful analysis of the project.

AAR Template

What was supposed to happen?
What did happen?
Sustains:
1.
2.
3.
Improves:
1.
2.
3.

Calculate project ROI

ROI stands for Return on Investment, and is commonly used by investors to determine if they're making the right choices with their money. However, ROI is not only applicable to investing. Everything in business (and life) has a return on investment. For simple processes like buying Facebook ads that lead people through a sales funnel to buy one of your products, calculating ROI is simple (see example below). However, for more complex, creative, or non-linear actions (say, buying a cup of coffee to help you produce more content faster, or the choice to use preexisting software instead of engineering your own solution), measuring results can be much harder. In this section, I'm going to briefly run through how to calculate ROI for a digital, collaborative project, and explain why you and your collaborators should have this talk, whether the results are positive or not.

How to calculate ROI

According to Investopedia:

"ROI = (gain from investment - cost of investment) / cost of investment"

The answer is always a percentage or ratio.[1]

For collaborative processes, the calculation is a bit more complicated. We need to calculate the revenue of the project, total expenses (like overhead, software, etc.), and, to get a clear picture of how we're doing, we need to calculate time investment of each collaborator, specifically relative to what a single hour of his or her time is worth.

The collaborative ROI calculator looks like this:

Collaborative ROI = (((project revenue + potential future return) - (project expenses + (value of hour of time*total collaborators))/(project expenses + (value of hour of time*total collaborators))

In order to calculate ROI effectively, you'll need to analyze the three elements of your 1-1-1 Product Launch Method, calculating expenses and time investment for each part, as well as calculating total time investment of each group member in relation to what an hour of their time is worth.

While this sounds complicated, we're not looking for a hard and fast answer, but a sort of ruler we can use to measure the effectiveness of our efforts and the launch. I'll walk you through the High Speed Elite case study to show you how we calculated ROI.

Case Study: Calculating ROI for High Speed Elite

Step 1. Calculate money investment on Lead Generation, Lead Capture, and Lead Conversion

During our first launch for High Speed Elite, we had a very limited audience. While John and Antonio had built audiences into the hundreds of thousands, they weren't specifically audiences of veterans. That meant that marketing our new program to any of their hundreds of thousands of listeners or readers wouldn't bring in many new potential customers, so we had to find another Lead Generator. We focused on Facebook ads.

We invested $458.79 for a total of 66 email opt-ins on our Lead Capture Page. Each collaborator also emailed their list, and posted on social media our new program for veterans (effectively no money investment here as they already had email lists and this would not accrue additional cost). I spent extra time connecting with individual veterans I knew, sending direct, personalized emails to each of them. This is a time investment, which we'll calculate later.

For our Lead Capture, we set up a simple optin page using Optimizepress.com, which cost $97. We hooked it up to an email marketing system, which you can get for free through Mailchimp. Because I created all the copy and images for the main page, this is all we invested in this process.

For Lead Conversion, we ran a webinar. We used GotoWebinar, which is expensive, but Antonio already used this in his business. You can run a webinar for free through Google Hangout, however, but may need to pay extra for a good chatbox so you can get people interacting. Chatroll costs $20. Because I created the slides and kept them simple, there was no additional expense for conversion. I also followed up with many of the students through one on one calls, but calls were made via skype, so that was free as well (minus time investment, which we'll cover in the next part).

Hosting for the website cost us about $10 per month, or about $120 for the first year (the time we would need it up and operating to test our launch).

All in, we spent about $695.79.

Step 2. Calculate total expenses to build your MVP

Our MVP was nothing more than an outline that we presented on the webinar. We had agreed not to build anything unless 5 students signed up at our introductory price. If less joined, we would have either refunded all presale money (we let all students know this was the case, so it would not have been a surprise) or made the collective decision to move forward regardless, even if it meant going into the red.

I created the slides on PowerPoint, but you could use Google Slides, which is free, so our effective total expenses for building our MVP was $0.00.

Step 3. Calculate time investment for all parties

This is where calculating ROI becomes a bit more tricky. Expenses are hard and fast and it's easy to determine how much money you paid to produce something versus what you made from selling it. With time, our most valuable commodity, it's not so easy.

There are two ways to do this. First, you can define a dollar amount that you believe you're worth per hour. For example: $30 per hour. Then you can simply multiple total hours you spent on the project times this amount. Have all collaborators do the same and add to total expenses to determine cost of investment.

Alternatively, you can calculate revenue after expenses for the project and then divide by total hours spent by all collaborators to see what an average time of work was worth to all of you. In my opinion, this is a better ruler for measuring than putting an arbitrary dollar figure to a single hour of time.

Unfortunately, for our project, I'm the only person who tracked my time down to the hour (I used a great free tool called Toggl that you can access at Toggl.com), but I can estimate my collaborator's time investment as well.

We launched end of August 2014, and closed the carts in September of 2014. Our launch window was approximately 10 days, with two live webinars to get our first class together.

Leading up to launch and the close of the carts, I invested 128 hours. Post launch, I invested another 60 hours to mentor, train, and build the training platform, courses, and other resources. I estimate that our group as a whole invested a total of 350 hours (I was lead on this project, and time and hustle were the superpowers I brought to the group, hence why not everyone had to nor needed to invest so much time).

My time tracker through Toggl:

Total 182:37:39
Export
0:00
0:00
2:39
4:30
3:01
13:38
33:49
55:31
29:25
20:04
11:54
8:01
January 2014
February 2014
March 2014
April 2014
May 2014
June 2014
July 2014
August 2014
September 2014
October 2014
November 2014
December 2014
Grouped by Project / Time Entry
Sorted by Title (A - z)
HSLD
182:37:39

Step 4. Calculate ROI (without time investment)

We earned approximately $19,738.00 at launch. Several purchases were made over a 6 month period, but to keep calculation a bit simpler, we'll assume all funds were paid up front. Assuming a bank processing fee of 3%, this would be $19,145.86.

High Speed Elite ROI = (Gain from Investment - Cost of Investment) / Cost of Investment

High Speed Elite ROI = ($19,145.86 - $695.79) / $695.79

High Speed Elite ROI = $18,450.07 / $695.79

High Speed Elite ROI = 26.52*100% (to make it a percentage)

ROI = 2,652%

Effectively, we turned $695.79 into $18,450.07 for an ROI of 2,652%.

Wow, insane! We should launch projects every day!

Not so fast.

Now it's time to determine time investment, and what every person's time was worth on this.

Step 5. Calculate ROI including time investment

Now take your total Gain from Investment less the Cost of Investment, and divide by total hours spent on the project.

$18,450.07 / 350 hours = $52.17 / hour

So for every hour invested in this project, we made about $52.17. While a decent hourly rate, it's also just an estimate. I'm not calculating additional investments made beyond the launch at this point. This would assume that everything was built and we could walk away from the project, but that wasn't the case. We ended up investing about $10,000 more into the project to build the platform, create the training material, and mentor and train our students (helping build and design their websites, helping them with product creation and distribution, etc.).

If you remove the post-launch investment of $10,000, you're left with $8,450.07 (or approximately 179% ROI). Divide that by 350 hours and you get $24.14 / hour.

While not as great as $52 / hour, or a 2,652% ROI, it's still profitable. What's really important to realize here, though, is that we did this on a limited budget with limited investment. We did not have to take out bank loans. We did not need an angel investor who would subsequently take 50% of our profit. We did not have to quit our full time jobs to do this. Each of us was working part time on this project (300 hours between 3 people, spread over 6 months is approximately 16 hours of work per month per person, or two full work days of work. Think about it...).

By collaborating, we were able to build something from scratch and make it profitable relatively quickly. More importantly, it set us up for future launches.

Step 6. Calculate future potential profit

Here is the real beauty of collaboration: not only have we bootstrapped to profitability, but we now have an asset we can relaunch with less time, money and effort.

Calculating future potential profit is difficult. There are dozens, if not hundreds, of variables. But assuming you can launch your program again, generate the same or better revenue, with less time and money investment, you will dramatically increase your overall ROI on the project.

We decided to relaunch High Speed Elite again six months later. We generated more revenue with less investment (below $5,000) and less time investment (about 100 hours). I estimate our second launch ROI was over 500%, for an average of about 340% ROI.

Summary

This is the power of collaboration, the power of digital product launches, and the power of scalability; we can now continue to relaunch this program into the future because it's built and the systems are in place, we just have to invest a little time, money, and sweat equity to generate leads and close sales (a very marginal cost).

Calculate Money investment on Lead Generation, Lead Capture, and Lead Conversion
Calculate total expenses to build your MVP
Calculate time investment for all parties
Calculate ROI without time investment
Calculate ROI including time investment
Calculate future potential profit

Determine next steps

You've successfully launched your product. Now what?

First and foremost, you need to deliver on your promises. If you presold a product or service, you need to put all your effort into delighting your early adopters. And you owe it to them—they invested in something unproven, even though they didn't have to. That's a remarkable vote of confidence, and you should not take that for granted.

Beyond delivering on your promise, you'll need to make a few choices. In this section, I'll outline common questions and concerns, and ways to approach each one individually and as a collaboration.

Should we continue to work together?

Success or failure, this should be a topic for conversation. If you drafted up a contract, there's a good chance it was only for the initial project. This means you'll need to re-engage with your collaborators to determine if they want to move forward with the project beyond the established timelines and deliverables.

Questions you should discuss with your collaborators:

Focus	Questions	Answer
Should we continue to collaborate?	Was everyone satisfied with the project—both working with one another and the product itself?	
	If we continued to work together, what would that look like?	

Re-launch or next project?	If we do not want to continue working together, what is a simple, mutually beneficial way to break off this engagement?	
	If only some of the collaborators do not want to work continue, how do we plan to fill their roles? Do we need to take on new roles and responsibilities? Are we okay with that?	
	Have we built something that we can roll out again in the future with minimal investment?	
	How far can we take this project? How many students, customers, etc.?	
	Can we improve or expand our current project for a second launch?	
	What would make us change directions or start a new project? What criteria is worth looking into and discussing to come to a decision?	
	What would the next launch look like?	
Timeline	What is a plausible timeline for our next launch?	
	Who can commit to this timeline?	
	Are there factors we aren't taking into consideration? What are we not considering that we should?	

Going your separate ways after a collaborative project

Danny Iny, founder of Mirasee, formerly Firepole Marketing, began his business with a collaborative partner, Peter. However, as time went on, priorities shifted: "We started looking at [our collaborative business] in 2010. Not that much later Peter had his first child, a son, and he was juggling a whole bunch of projects like I was. His priorities shifted, as children are likely to do to one's priorities, and he had less to devote to [our collaborative project]. We finally had to acknowledge that [the collaboration] was no longer an alignment of direction and interest and focus, and we have to go our separate ways professionally."

It's important to realize that neither Danny nor Peter had hard feelings about this eventual split. Events happen in life that can shift our focus and our priorities. By maintaining an open, transparent discourse, you can better manage these inevitable shifts.

Azimuth Check

After your product launch, it's important to conduct your After Action Review. Discuss with your collaborators what went right, what went wrong, where you can sustain your successes and where you can improve your performance. Use the AAR format to open up communication with everyone involved on the project. Next, determine your Return on Investment of your collaborative project. After doing the honest calculations, was the project worth your time? Whether yes or no, sit down with your collaborators to discuss follow up steps and whether you should work together again, on a relaunch of the same project or on a new project, or go your separate ways. Keep this conversation professional and avoid personal critiques—whether a success or failure, collaboration has many positive ramifications and it's always more beneficial to all parties if you end working together on a positive note.

Take a short break here to take notes or add your thoughts below before moving onto the next section:

THE *COLLABORATE* PLAYBOOK

Whether you're a struggling solopreneur, or part of a successful team (or somewhere in between), here is the step-by-step playbook to assemble, organize, and lead a small team of creative collaborators to create, market, and launch digital products online:

PHASE 1: FUEL

MILESTONE 1: Understand Collaboration

- ✓ Define collaboration
- ✓ Overcome common negative myths of collaboration
- ✓ Understand the solution to these myths and how to apply collaboration to your project

MILESTONE 2: Develop the Collaboration Mindset

- ✓ Understand mindset and belief and how they relate to collaboration
- ✓ Overcome common limiting beliefs about business and collaboration
- ✓ Implement the "Collaboration Mindset" into your life and work

MILESTONE 3: Define What You Want

- ✓ Discover what makes you tick

- ✓ Define your definition of success
- ✓ Determine the ideal lifestyle you want to live

MILESTONE 4: Define What You Offer

- ✓ Define and understand your unique value
- ✓ Understand how you are different than others and why it matters
- ✓ Define where your unique value can provide the most value to other collaborators

PHASE 2: ASSEMBLE

MILESTONE 5: Develop Your Profitable Idea

- ✓ Brainstorm possible potential products or services
- ✓ Use the Profitable Idea Framework to mitigate the downside risk of choosing an unprofitable idea
- ✓ Conduct your idea summary and decide on what idea you plan to move forward with

MILESTONE 6: Define Your Ideal Collaborator

- ✓ Understand the characteristics of an effective collaborator
- ✓ Define your ideal collaborator
- ✓ Use the Portfolio Metric to refine your search

MILESTONE 7: Build Your Team

- ✓ Develop a list of potential collaborators
- ✓ Connect with your ideal collaborator
- ✓ Decide to move forward or keep looking

PHASE 3: CREATE

MILESTONE 8: Set the Foundation for Collaborative Success

- ✓ Establish your working agreement
- ✓ Establish roles, responsibilities, scope of work, and project parameters
- ✓ Mitigate early team risk through agreements and conflict resolution strategy development

MILESTONE 9: Plan Your Project

- ✓ Build your one page business model
- ✓ Define your Minimum Viable Product
- ✓ Create your marketing and product wireframe

MILESTONE 10: Develop Your Product

- ✓ Define Objectives, Task Lists, and create your timeline
- ✓ Understand the 80/20 principle and how to apply it to your project
- ✓ Manage your team to stay on track

PHASE 4: LAUNCH

MILESTONE 11: Create Your Sales Funnel

- ✓ Understand what makes people buy
- ✓ Build your sales funnel
- ✓ Begin marketing

MILESTONE 12: Pre-Sell Your Product

- ✓ Conduct a dry run rehearsal

- ✓ Feed the funnel
- ✓ Close the sale

PHASE 5: ACCELERATE

MILESTONE 13: Onboard New Customers

- ✓ Conduct new user onboarding
- ✓ Crowdsource product development
- ✓ Iteratively deliver your product

MILESTONE 14: Review, Evaluate, Improve, Grow

- ✓ Conduct your After Action Review
- ✓ Calculate project Return on Investment
- ✓ Determine next steps for your collaboration

CONCLUSION

Congratulations. You've completed *Collaborate*, and, therefore, you've collaboratively built and launched a product from scratch. Whether success or failure (or somewhere in between), this is a huge accomplishment. Very few people consider building something worthwhile without being told to by their boss; fewer ship. You did, and that's remarkable.

Also, the simple fact that you've read this far says a lot about you. First, it puts you in the top percentile of readers in the world. According to Statistic Brain Research Institute, 80% of U.S. families did not buy a book last year. Even worse, 42% of college students will never read a book again after they graduate.[1] I assume these statistics would be even more depressing if you included the rest of the world and accounted for those without degrees.

But not you.

This means you're already way beyond your peers, and that you have a leg up on the competition. This is an important edge; don't take it for granted.

Second, it means you value your time, money, and effort, and you see the value in teaming up with others to build and launch worthwhile products. Again, this sets you apart from the millions of others who would rather not attempt the hard, creative work you're doing. This is exactly why you will succeed and flourish where they fail and recede.

Remember, reading is only useful if you put your knowledge to work. With this book, you know how it works, and you have a framework that I wish I had before I started this journey. You also have my support. If you have any questions, you can email me: Tom@insurgentpublishing.com, and I'll help you (I mean that sincerely); but I can't do the work for you. That's still on you and always will be.

My call to action for you: Go now and launch something.

Don't wait until tomorrow, it never comes.

Start today. Start before you're ready. Very soon, you will be.

Good luck, and I'll see you in the fray...

Tom Morkes, CEO of Insurgent Publishing

NOTES

Introduction

1. https://gigaom.com/2010/05/31/work-better-by-seeking-out-competition/
2. http://www.spring.org.uk/2009/06/social-facilitation-how-and-when-audiences-improve-performance.php
3. http://www.theguardian.com/books/2012/nov/24/nassim-taleb-antifragile-finance-interview

PHASE 1: FUEL

MILESTONE 1: Understand Collaboration

1. http://www.investopedia.com/terms/n/net_margin.asp

MILESTONE 2: Develop the Collaboration Mindset

1. http://mashable.com/2014/01/30/startup-success-infographic/#i_dbA25c9gqr
2. http://www.sciencedirect.com/science/article/pii/S0167811612000584

PHASE 2: ASSEMBLE

MILESTONE 5: Develop Your Profitable Idea

1. http://venturehacks.com/articles/minimum-viable-product

PHASE 3: CREATE

MILESTONE 9: Plan Your Project

1. https://www.blueoceanstrategy.com/what-is-blue-ocean-strategy/

2. http://steveblank.com/2015/05/06/build-measure-learn-throw-things-against-the-wall-and-see-if-they-work/
3. http://leanstack.com/about/
4. https://publishizer.com/collaborate/

MILESTONE 10: Develop Your Product

1. http://whatis.techtarget.com/definition/kanban
2. https://www.computer.org/csdl/proceedings/afips/1959/5055/00/50550160.pdf

PHASE 4: LAUNCH

MILESTONE 11: Create Your Sales Funnel

1. http://www.cbsnews.com/news/iphone-6-fans-line-up-a-week-before-apple-unveils-it/
2. http://www.cnet.com/news/four-of-apples-biggest-missteps-from-maps-to-mobileme/
3. http://www.entrepreneur.com/article/244019
4. http://www.ted.com/talks/j_j_abrams_mystery_box#t-328115
5. http://nathanbarry.com/launchfail/
6. Robert Cialdini, *Influence: The Psychology of Persuasion* (Collins, 1993), 211.
7. http://nathanbarry.com/urgency/
8. http://www.researchgate.net/publication/229126990_Are_scarce_products_always_more_attractive_The_interaction_of_different_types_of_scarcity_signals_with_products%27_suitability_for_conspicuous_consumption
9. http://psycnet.apa.org/journals/psp/32/5/906/
10. Paco Underhill, *Why We Buy: The Science of Shopping* (Simon & Schuster, 1999), 220.
11. http://searchengineland.com/2013-study-79-of-consumers-trust-online-reviews-as-much-as-personal-recommendations-164565
12. http://www.ncbi.nlm.nih.gov/pubmed/22869334
13. http://www.ringdna.com/inside-sales-glossary/what-is-the-sales-funnel
14. http://www.slideshare.net/dmc500hats/startup-metrics-for-pirates-seedcamp-2008-presentation
15. Justin Mares, Traction: A Startup Guide to Getting Customers (S-curves Publishing, 2014), 288.

MILESTONE 12: Pre-Sell Your Product

1. Eric Ries, *The Lean Startup: How Today's Entrepreneurs Use Continuous Innovation to Create Radically Successful Businesses* (Crown Business, 2011), 149.

PHASE 5: ACCELERATE

MILESTONE 13: Onboard New Customers

1. https://en.wikipedia.org/wiki/Onboarding#Limits_and_criticisms_of_onboarding_theory
2. http://www.merriam-webster.com/dictionary/crowdsourcing
3. http://www.merriam-webster.com/dictionary/iteration
4. http://www.forbes.com/sites/ciocentral/2014/04/08/silicon-valley-isnt-innovative-its-iterative-four-proof-points/

MILESTONE 14: Review, Evaluate, Improve, Grow

1. http://www.investopedia.com/terms/r/returnoninvestment.asp

Conclusion

1. http://www.statisticbrain.com/reading-statistics/

ACKNOWLEDGEMENTS

First and foremost, thank you to everyone who helped with the creation of this book: Courtney, for putting up with me while I wrestled with this topic for over a year; Guy Vincent for cajouling me to use Publishizer.com so I could fund my book before I started writing; Tom Owens for the developmental editing; Chris O'Byrne and JETLAUNCH.net for the interior design and formatting; Ari Vik for the jacket design and cover art; Harry Copeman for the cover concept design; Mary for essentially rewriting this book about five times with me, acting as producer and editor to clean up all my painful grammar and spelling mistakes, and making sure the whole thing flowed intuitively; and, again, to all the people who pre-ordered on Publishizer.com when this book was nothing more than an idea and a promise.

Thank you to all the people who were kind enough to let me interview them or pick their brain about collaboration, business, and building digital products, including: Martyn Bromley, Guy Vincent, Corbett Barr, Jon Nastor, Kira Slye, Chris Guillebeau, Danny Iny, Matt Helbig,, AJ Leon, Chris Ducker, Sean Ogle, Dan Norris, Justin McGill, CPT. Mark Aalderink, Omar Bradley, Reg Seeton, Nathan Barry, and Paul Boyce. In particular, I'd like to recognize Lawrence Green whose friendship and conversation helped me shape and form Milestone's 2 through 8, specifically in regards to how we ought to approach collaboration, why mindset is so important, and how we can begin to shape our relationships and plans to start collaborating most effectively. I couldn't have written this book without your insight Lawrence - thank you.

Thanks to all the people whose writing and ideas have inspired the work I do today and have, in some way, directly or indirectly, impacted the words on these pages: Nassim Taleb, Seth Godin, Steven Pressfield, Ash Maurya, Eric Ries, Clayton M. Christensen, Geoffrey A. Moore, Peter Thiel, Richard Koch, Michael Masterson, Dan Ariely, Tim Ferriss, Daniel H. Pink, Robert B. Cialdini, and Chip and Dan Heath.

Thank you to all the people whose great work, and in many cases, mentorship and friendship, inspired me to write this book in the first place. In no particular order (because you're all number one): John Lee Dumas, Antonio Centeno, Jonathan Mead, Elisa Doucette, Jeff Goins, Taylor Pearson, Jason Spencer, Al Pittampalli, Tommy Walker, Clay Hebert, Jennifer Blanchard, Dan Adams, John Corcoran, Benjamin Jenks, Nate Kutsko, Dave Ursillo, Cliff Ravenscraft, Jason Andrew Bond, Ryan Hanley, Rachel Gilliam, Ryan Levesque, Matthew Scott, Dr. Jason Winkle, Joshua Rivers, Dr. Lee Warren, Sean McCabe, Dane Maxwell, Bryan Harris, Max Altschuler, Sujan Patel, Justin Sloan, Kevin Kermes, Trevor Scott, Tyson Adams, Will Lenzen Jr., Bjork Ostrom, and Jeff Rose.

And finally, thank you to all the entrepreneurs, writers, artists, investors, warriors, and leaders I've gotten to know and collaborate with over the last few years, including all of my private coaching clients, the veterans who took the plunge to join *High Speed Elite*, the founding members of *The Flight Formula*, the artists and writers who collaborated on *The Creative Entrepreneur* and *Bootstrapped*, the authors and publishers I've mentored inside *Publishers' Empire*, and all the authors, editors, designers, and publishers I've been blessed to work with through *Insurgent Publishing:* your support and confidence gives my work meaning, and the great work you do continues to inspire and motivate me to keep doing what I do; thank you.

ABOUT THE AUTHOR

Tom Morkes is the founder and CEO of InsurgentPublishing.com, the co-founder of HighSpeedLowDrag.org, the creator of PublishersEmpire.com, the host of the podcast "In the Trenches," the author of four books, including *The Complete Guide to Pay What You Want Pricing,* and a co-creator and collaborator on dozens of other creative and business projects. His work has been described as "amazing," "prolific," and "the best thing since sliced bread."

In a former life, Tom graduated from The United States Military Academy with a double major in Russian and Human Geography, deployed to Iraq as a Gun Truck Convoy Security Platoon Leader, and even got paid to jump out of helicopters for a while. With essentially zero employable skills, Tom was forced into entrepreneurship at the ripe age of 27. With nothing more than a laptop and a pair of around-the-world plane tickets, Tom and his wife Courtney proceeded to travel the globe for 24 months while collaborating and launching digital products online.

The world (and the internet) hasn't been the same since.

You can reach Tom on Twitter @tmorkes, at his blog TomMorkes.com, or at participating indie coffee shops and micro-breweries around the world.

CPSIA information can be obtained
at www.ICGtesting.com
Printed in the USA
LVOW03*0837280216
476991LV00001B/1/P

9 781940 715049